剑川沙溪古镇二十年图志

Twenty Years of Jianchuan Shaxi Ancient Town Pictorial Annals

剑川县地方志编纂委员会办公室 编

Drafted by Jianchuan Local Pictorial Annals Codification Committee Office

方志出版社

Publishing House of Local Records

图书在版编目（CIP）数据

剑川沙溪古镇二十年图志 / 剑川县地方志编纂委员会办公室编. -- 北京 : 方志出版社，2021.12
ISBN 978-7-5144-5029-3

Ⅰ. ①剑… Ⅱ. ①剑… Ⅲ. ①乡镇 – 地方史 – 剑川县 – 图集 Ⅳ. ①K297.45-64

中国版本图书馆CIP数据核字(2022)第100593号

责任编辑 程 倩
责任校对 刘玉霞
责任印制 赵 楚
出 版 者 方志出版社
地 址 北京市朝阳区潘家园东里9号（国家方志馆4层）
邮 编 100021
网 址 http: //www.zgfzcb.cn
发 行 方志出版社图书营销中心（010-67110500）
印 刷 云南美嘉美印刷包装有限公司
开 本 889毫米 × 1250毫米 1/16
印 张 21.25
字 数 435千字
版 次 2021年12月第1版
印 次 2021年12月第1次印刷
定 价 680.00元

《剑川沙溪古镇二十年图志》编纂人员

顾　　问：李增堂　张茂兴　颜寿红

主　　编：李德琦

副 主 编：苏生林　董静海　段泽宣

执行副主编：段泽宣

图片供稿：苏金泉　赵爱春　黄印武　杨惠铭　张龙福
段力刚　史玉培　钱昌云　汪静蓉　张琴兰
赵泰元　杨富宝　陈凤媛　王观远　赵子忠

编　　审：陈天武　代燕春　王超英　雷家彬　那　鹏
李建川　张　笑　欧阳子龙　刘文忠　杨应宇
杨毅松　陈劲锟　黄印武　张龙福　张燮举
杨树林　赵爱春　史玉培

特邀编纂单位：云南美嘉美印刷包装有限公司

Editorial Personnel of "Twenty Years of Jianchuan Shaxi Ancient Town Pictorial Annals"

Consultant: Li Zengtang, Zhang Maoxing, Yan Shouhong

Chief Editor: Li Deqi

Associate Editor: Su Shenglin, Dong Jinghai, Duan Zexuan

Executive Associate Editor: Duan Zexuan

Pictures Provider: Su Jinquan, Zhao Aichun, Huang Yinwu,
Yang Huiming, Zhang Longfu,
Duan Ligang, Shi Yupei, Qian Changyun,
Wang Jingrong, Zhang Cuilan,
Zhao Taiyuan, Yang Fubao,
Chen Fengyuan, Wang Guanyuan,
Zhao Zizhong

Copy Editor: Chen Tianwu, Dai Yanchun, Wang Chaoying,
Lei Jiabin, Na Peng, Li Jianchuan,
Zhang Xiao, Ouyang Zilong, Liu Wenzhong,
Yang Yingyu,Yang Yisong, Chen Jinkun,
Huang Yinwu, Zhang Longfu, Zhang Xieju,
Yang Shulin, Zhao Aichun, Shi Yupei

Invited Compiler: Yunnan Meijiamei Printing and Packaging Co., Ltd.

序

作为滇藏茶马古道的重要驿站，沙溪古镇是运送和交易茶叶、药材、丝织品以及盐的重镇，在历史上一直发挥着举足轻重的作用。随着19世纪末现代公路网络的完善和交通工具的发展，茶马古道逐渐淡出历史舞台，沙溪古镇失去了往日的繁华。然而，当地具有约600年历史的古戏台、马店、四方街、兴教寺等得以完整保留，最终成为宝贵的文化遗产。

2001年沙溪寺登街被世界纪念性建筑基金会（WMF）选入“2002年值得关注的101个世界濒危建筑遗产名录”。2003年开始实施的中国·瑞士合作“沙溪复兴工程”，致力于沙溪的文化保护与可持续发展，主要包括保护文化遗产、改善基础设施、保护文化景观和建立经济发展的多样性等方面。

2003—2020年，借助五期沙溪复兴工程的实施，沙溪镇进一步提升了在国内外的知名度，沙溪这个“茶马古道上唯一幸存的古集市”逐步恢复了昔日的繁华，成为中外游客的旅游目的地，为打造地方文化旅游品牌、发展民族文化旅游和促进当地经济社会的可持续发展起到了积极作用。

2015年以来，沙溪镇先后开展了国家建制镇示范试点、国家新型城镇化综合试点等工作；2017年，沙溪镇被住房和城乡建设部列为第二批全国特色小镇；2018年，沙溪镇被列为云南省15个特色小镇之一，获得省级奖补资金2.6亿元。在特色小镇创建过程中，沙溪古镇牢固树立“绿水青山就是金山银山”的发展理念，科学布局古镇生产、生活、生态空间，统筹“产城人文”融合发展，保护田园风光，挖掘文化内涵，彰显乡愁特色，创新智慧建设，推动生态保护与旅游发展互促共融、新型城镇化与旅游业有机结合，将美丽资源转化为“美丽经济”，打造生态优美、宜居宜业宜游、智慧便捷的健康生活目的地。

沙溪复兴工程成功走出了贫困地区创新城镇投融资体制、“变废为宝”、保护利用与群众脱贫致富相结合的可持续发展之路。在特色小镇创建中，沙溪秉承“保护、发展”的理念，深化与瑞士苏黎世联邦理工学院的合作，依托瑞士先进的国际理念，有效总结以中瑞合作沙溪复兴工程推动旅游发展、乡村振兴、文化自信、新型城镇化等方面的经验，使之成为国内国际示范典范的经验，推动沙溪按国际化标准高品质推进建设和持续健康发展。

随着国家方志馆南方丝绸之路分馆落户大理剑川古城，作为中国历史文化名镇的沙溪古镇是南方丝绸之路中外文化交流的实物见证之一，为更好地服务国家方志馆南方丝绸之路分馆的建设，让更多国内外各界人士能直观、全面地领略沙溪古镇优美的自然风光，了解其悠久的历史文化，使更多的人知晓沙溪、来到沙溪、共享沙溪之美，剑川县地方志编纂委员会办公室编纂出版了《剑川沙溪古镇二十年图志》。图志创新志书编排方式，以图文并茂的形式，生动直观地展示了沙溪古镇2001—2020年二十年的经济社会发展变化。这是一项很有价值，也很有意义的工作！

回顾历史，豪情满怀；继往开来，信心倍增。站在新的起点上，沙溪必将以更加昂扬的姿态阔步向前。

剑川县地方志编纂委员会办公室

2021年12月

Prologue

Being an important courier station on the Yunnan-Xizang Historic Tea and Horse Caravan Trail, Shaxi Ancient Town is a strategic town for the transportation and transaction of tea, herbal medicine, silk and salt, and has been playing a pivotal role in history. With the development of modern road networks and transportation in the late 19th century, the Historic Tea and Horse Caravan Trail has gradually fade from the historical stage, and Shaxi Ancient Town also was not as prosperous as before. However, those local architectures with roughly 600 years history, such as Ancient Opera Stages, Caravansaries, Sifang Street, Xingjiao Temple and etc. got to preserved intactly, and finally became a precious culture heritage.

In 2001, the Shaxi Sideng Street was listed in the "World Monuments Watch List of 101 Most Endangered Sites in 2002" by the World Monuments Fund (WMF), Shaxi finally reborn in a different way. The Shaxi Rehabilitation Project cooperated between China and Switzerland started from 2003 is dedicated to Shaxi's cultural protection and sustainable development, this mainly includes the protection of cultural heritage, the development of infrastructure, the protection of cultural landscape and the establishment of economic development diversity etc.

During 2003-2020, through the implementation of 5 stages' Shaxi Rehabilitation Project, Shaxi Town further improves its domestic and overseas popularity. Being the "only ancient market survived on the Historic Tea and Horse Caravan Trail, Shaxi has gradually restored its former prosperity, and has become a traveling destiny for tourists from domestic and abroad, and also caused a positive effect on building local cultural tourism brand, developing national cultural tourism and promoting the sustainable development of local economy and society.

Since 2015, Shaxi Town has carried out pilot projects for nationally organized towns and comprehensive pilot projects for new-type urbanization. In 2017, Shaxi Town was rated by the Ministry of Housing and Urban-Rural Development as one of the national Specialty Small Towns (Batch 2). In 2018, Shaxi Town was listed as one of the 15 Specialty Small Towns of Yunnan Province and won 260 million RMB of provincial awards. During the establish period of Specialty Small Town, Shaxi Town firmly uphold the development philosophy that "Lucid Waters and Lush Mountains Are Invaluable Assets", and distribute production, living and ecological space scientifically, coordinating a combining development of "City Production and Humanity", preserving countryside scenery and digging culture nature, demonstrating the characteristics of homesickness, innovating intelligent construction, promoting the integration of ecological protection and tourism development and the organic integration of new urbanization and tourism, transferring beautiful resources into "Beautiful Economics", and building a healthy living destination with beautiful ecology, suitable for living, working and tourisms and with intelligence and convenience.

The Shaxi Rehabilitation Project has successfully achieved a sustainable developing path of the masses shake off poverty and get rich combined with the innovative urban investment and financing system of poverty area, turning waste into wealth, protection and utilization. During the construction of Specialty Small Town, Shaxi has been adhering the idea of "Protect and Development", deepen the cooperation with Switzerland, relying on the advanced international idea of Switzerland to efficiently summary the experience from the tourism development, rural revitalization, culture confidence, new urbanization promoted by China-Switzerland Shaxi Rehabilitation Project, and making it become the experience in domestic and international examples, and further promoting the construction and sustainable and sound development of Shaxi as high quality international standard.

With the "Southern Silk Road" branch museum of National Local Chronicles Museum established in Jianchuan Ancient Town of Dali, Shaxi Ancient Town, being a famous Chinese historical culture town, is the physical witness of the culture communication between China and foreign countries through "Southern Silk Road". In order to better service the construction of the "Southern Silk Road" branch museum of National Local Chronicles Museum, and letting more domestic and international personnel have a visualized and comprehensive view of the beautiful scenery of Shaxi Ancient Town and its historic culture, and to know Shaxi and come to Shaxi and enjoy the beauty of Shaxi, Jianchuan Local Pictorial Annals Codification Committee Office drafted and published the "Twenty Years of Jianchuan Shaxi Ancient Town Pictorial Annals". It made an innovation on the layout manner and use text and pictures to vividly illustrate the changes of development for the Shaxi Ancient Town's economic society during 2001-2020. This is a very valuable and meaningful work and shall be congratulated for the successful publishment of it.

We are full of pride when looking back on history, we will carry the past and move forward with greater confidence. Standing on a new start, Shaxi will stride forward with a more high-spirited attitude.

Jianchuan Local Pictorial Annals Codification Committee Office

December 2021

凡　例

一、本图志坚持以马克思列宁主义、毛泽东思想、邓小平理论、“三个代表”重要思想、科学发展观、习近平新时代中国特色社会主义思想为指导，坚持辩证唯物主义和历史唯物主义的立场、观点和方法，存真求实，力求全面、客观、系统地记述剑川沙溪镇2001—2020年的历史和发展进程。

二、本图志参照志书编排原则，志首设概述、大事记；正文设9章；志末设后记。

三、本图志记述时限上起2001年，下至2020年。为保持事物的连续性和完整性，个别事物的记述时限适当上溯。记述中按照详今略古、详近略远的原则进行编修。

四、本图志正文采用章节体。

五、本图志以现代语体文记述，行文按《地方志书质量规定》和《云南省第二轮地方志编纂行文规定》要求，力求文风严谨、朴实，语言简洁、流畅。

六、本图志随文配图，图下设文字说明。

七、本图志使用的各项数据主要以县统计局提供的数据为准，数据缺乏的采用主管部门或主办单位正式提供的数据。

八、本图志标点符号、数字用法、计量单位分别执行国家标准《标点符号用法》（GB/T 15834—2011）、《出版物上数字用法》（GB/T 15835—2011）和《中华人民共和国法定计量单位》。

九、本图志纪年，中华人民共和国成立前采用历史纪年，括注公元纪年。

General Notices

1. This pictorial annals follows the guidance of Marxism-Leninism, Mao Zedong Thought, Deng Xiaoping Theory, the Important Thought of "Three Represents", the Scientific Outlook on Development, and Xi Jinping Thought on Socialism with Chinese Characteristics for a New Era, adhere to the positions, viewpoints, and methods of dialectical and historical materialism, to strive to describe the history and development process of Shaxi Town of Jianchuan County during 2001-2020 in a comprehensive, objective and systematic manner.

2. This pictorial annals refers to the choreography principles of annals, sets general introduction, chronicles in the beginning, the main text consist of 9 chapters, and set afterword at the end.

3. This pictorial annals recording period is from 2001 to 2020. In order to keep the continuity and completeness of context, part of the contexts' recording period has been traced upstream properly. The record applies the principle of details the present and recent days while generalizes the old and ancient days.

4. The writing style of this pictorial annals is chapter style.

5. This pictorial annals describes in modern vernacular, in accordance with "The Requirements of the Quality Regulations of Local Chronicles" and "The Regulations on the Compilation of the Second Round of Local Chronicles in Yunnan Province", the writing style is rigorous, simple, and the language is concise and smooth.

6. This pictorial annals attached images along texts, with captions beneath images.

7. The data used in this pictorial annals is mainly based on the data provided by the County Statistics Bureau, and the missing data uses the data provided officially by the competent departments or sponsored authorities.

8. Punctuation marks, usage of numbers and units of measurement in this atlas are in accordance with the national standards "General Rules for Punctuation" (GB/T 15834—2011), "General Rules for Writing Numerals in Public Texts" (GB/T 15835—2011) and "Legal Units of Measurement of the People's Republic of China".

9. This pictorial annals counts the years and uses history annals before the establishment of the People's Republic of China with the common era noted in brackets.

目　录

Contents

概　述

沙溪镇位于中国云南剑川县西南部，地处大理、丽江、香格里拉之间，是一个以白族为主，彝族、汉族、傈僳族共居的多民族聚居镇。

沙溪头枕有“西南敦煌”之誉的石钟山，清幽细长的黑潓江从它的怀中蜿蜒流过，这里是古代通往南亚的重要国际通道，是“南方丝绸之路”的节点之一。沙溪古镇核心区寺登街位于坝子中心，是沙溪的政治、经济、文化中心，是从古到今沙溪贸易往来的集散地。远远望去，寺登街古树掩映，青瓦白墙，古朴清幽，“小桥流水人家”的景致秀美而雅致。这是“茶马古道”上唯一幸存的古集市，走进寺登街，便走进了那段“茶马古道”上马帮兴盛、商贸繁荣的历史。

2001年10月11日，世界纪念性建筑基金会（WMF）在美国纽约宣布：“中国沙溪寺登街（区域）是茶马古道上唯一幸存的古集市，有完整无缺的戏台、客栈、寺庙和寨门，使这个连接西藏和南亚的集市相当完备，入选2002年值得关注的101个世界濒危建筑遗产名录。”这使寺登街与埃及的国王谷、意大利的庞贝古城和万里长城齐名，被历史尘封的沙溪寺登街重新引起世人的关注和重视。

从2002年开始，剑川县人民政府和瑞士苏黎世联邦理工学院合作，致力于文化保护与可持续发展的沙溪复兴工程全面启动。复兴工程遵循国际文物修复的准则，用“修旧如旧、最少干预、最大保护”的理念复兴沙溪。复兴工程通过“四方街的修复、古村落的保护、沙溪坝的可持续发展、生态卫生系统的改造、脱贫致富与宣传”等不同的项目组成单元来实现区域规划。

复兴工程取得了阶段性的成绩，得到了国内外文化遗产保护部门的充分肯定。2005年，沙溪复兴项目获联合国教科文组织颁发的“亚太地区文化遗产保护杰出贡献奖”。茶马古道上这个唯一幸存的古集市，以完整、古朴的面容展现在世人面前，等待着国际国内与它有缘的人们来认识它、了解它、呵护它。

在国家部委，省州党委、政府的关心支持下，剑川县沙溪古镇于2017年被列入全省特色小镇创建名单，并被国家发改委列入第二批国家新型城镇化综合试点和新一轮特色小镇名单。沙溪特色小镇于2017年6月1日开工建设，累计完成投资14.36亿元。按照“一年见成效、两年基本完成、三年全面完成”的总体要求，突出重点、突出产业、突出特色，通过三年的努力，将沙溪镇建成全国一流、国际知名的国家级特色小镇。

独特的地理位置、温润的自然气候、秀美的田园风光、悠久的历史文化、浓郁的民族风情、令人惊叹的古代建筑，让沙溪拥有无限魅力。在特色小镇创建过程中，沙溪牢固树立“绿水青山就是金山银山”的发展理念，科学布局古镇生产、生活、生态空间，统筹“产城人文”融合发展，保护田园风光，挖掘文化内涵，彰显乡愁特色，创新智慧建设，推动生态保护与旅游发展互促共融、新型城镇化与旅游业有机结合，将美丽资源转化为“美丽经济”，打造生态优美、宜居宜业宜游、智慧便捷的健康生活目的地。沙溪已通过国家生态文明乡镇创建验收，被认定为云南省旅游名镇，石宝山—沙溪古镇创建为国家AAAA级旅游景区；2020年沙溪镇被中国旅游协会评为全国11个“最美小镇”之一，石宝山—沙溪古镇旅游景区被列入创建国家AAAAA级旅游景区重点推荐名单，沙溪成为剑川发展全域旅游的动力源。

近年，沙溪镇不断扩大对外开放，努力营造良好的投资环境，不断完善基础设施。“十三五”期间，镇党委、镇政府结合镇情，坚持“生态优先、民生为本、城镇活镇、农业稳镇、旅游兴镇、文化立镇、和谐安镇”的发展思路，坚决打好防范化解重大风险、精准脱贫、污染防治三大攻坚战，努力在脱贫攻坚、全域旅游、生态建设、乡村振兴、社会事业补短板、改革试点示范六个方面攻坚突破，促进全镇经济社会持续健康发展，努力构建“人文沙溪、生态沙溪、智慧沙溪”。在今后的工作中，沙溪镇将进一步解放思想，抢抓机遇，凝心聚力，开拓创新，狠抓落实，锁定“中国一流古镇”和“国际级旅游景点”的建设标准，着眼“大沙溪”的发展目标，努力把沙溪建设成为独具特色的旅游休闲型生态文明小镇。

General Introduction

Shaxi Town is in the southwest of Jianchuan County, Yunnan, China. This location is between Dali, Lijiang and Shangri-La, and it is a multi-ethnic town with Bai Nationality as the main group, Yi Nationality, Han Nationality and Lisu Nationality living together.

The front of Shaxi is the Shizhong Mountain, which is famous in the name of "Southwest Dunhuang", with slender Heihui River runs through it quietly. This place is an important ancient international corridor to South Asia and is also a joint point of the "Southern Silk Road". Sideng Street, the Core Area of Shaxi Ancient Town, is located in the middle of the basin, and is the political, economic and culture center of Shaxi, and also be the trading distribution center of Shaxi of all time. If we see from a distance, Sideng Street is shaded by ancient trees, with white walls and gray tiles, which is simple and quiet. The scenery of "Small Bridges, Flowing Water and Happy Family" is beautiful and elegant. This is the only ancient market survived on the "Historic Tea and Horse Caravan Trail". Walking into the Sideng Street means you walks into that thriving and prosperous history.

On October 11th, 2001, the World Monuments Fund (WMF) announced in New York of USA that "the Sideng Street (area) in Shaxi of China is the only Ancient Town survived on the "Historic Tea and Horse Caravan Trail". It has complete opera stages, hotels, temples and gates, these make this market connecting Xizang and South Asia a complete one and was selected into the list of "World Monuments Watch List of 101 Most Endangered Sites in 2002." This makes Sideng Street has the same reputation with Egypt's King Valley, Italy's Ancient City of Pompeii and the Great Wall from China. Although being sealed by history, Shaxi Sideng Street arouse the world's attention once again.

Since 2002, the government of Jianchuan County has been in cooperation with the Swiss Federal Institute of Technology in Zurich, and fully start the Shaxi Rehabilitation Project which is dedicated to culture protection and sustainable development. The rehabilitation project has been following the guidelines for international conservation of cultural relics and rehabilitate the Shaxi with the theory of "Repair the Old as Old, with Minimal Intervention to Achieve Maximum Preservation". With different project composition units, such as the renovation of Sifang Street, protection of ancient village, sustainable development of Shaxi Basin, transformation of the Eco-sanitation System and spreading of get rid of poverty and get rich, the rehabilitation project achieves the regional planning.

The rehabilitation project has achieved a stage achievement and was fully affirmed by cultural heritage protection departments from domestic and overseas. In 2005, the Shaxi Rehabilitation Project was awarded by UNESCO for "Award of Distinction, Asia-Pacific Heritage Awards for Cultural Heritage Conservation". This only ancient market survived on the "Historic Tea and Horse Caravan Trail" get to reveal itself completely and simply in front of the world, waiting for the people from domestic and overseas to come to recognize it, knows it and cares it.

With the care and support from national ministries, provincial and prefectural party committees and governments, the Shaxi Ancient Town of Jianchuan County has been listed on the list of the Specialty Small Town among whole province of 2017 and was also listed by the NDRC on the list of the second batch of national comprehensive trials for new urbanization and a new round of Specialty Small Town. The Specialty Small Town of Shaxi has started the construction on June 1st, 2017, and the total investment has reached 1.436 billion RMB. As per the general requirements of "One Year to See Performances, Two Years to Basically Complete, Three Years to Fully Complete", with the highlight, industries and specialties being emphasized, and through 3 years' efforts, established the Shaxi to a national first-class, internationally renowned national class Specialty Small Town.

With the unique geographical location, warm natural climate, beautiful pastoral scenery, long history and culture, rich ethnic customs and amazing ancient architecture, making Shaxi has infinite charms. During the construction process of Specialty Small Towns, Shaxi has been firmly attached to the developing theory of "Lucid Waters and Lush Mountains Are Invaluable Assets", and distribute production, living and ecological space scientifically, coordinating a combining development of "City Production and Humanity", preserving countryside scenery and digging culture nature, demonstrating the characteristics of homesickness, innovating intelligent construction, promoting the integration of ecological protection and tourism development and the organic integration of new urbanization and tourism, transferring beautiful resources into "Beautiful Economics", and building a healthy living destination with beautiful ecology, convenient for living, working and tourisms. Shaxi has passed the national ecological civilization township establishment acceptance and has been identified as a famous tourist town in Yunnan Province, with Mount Shibao-Shaxi Ancient Town was established as a National AAAA-Level Tourist Attraction; in 2020, Shaxi Town was rated by China Tourism Association as one of the 11th "Most Beautiful Small Town" in China. Mount Shibao-Shaxi Ancient Town Scenic Spot was listed in the key recommended list of National AAAAA-Level Tourist Attraction. Shaxi has become the power source for developing Jianchuan's full scale tourism.

In recent years, Shaxi Town continues to expand its opening to the outside world, striving to create a good investment environment and constantly improve its infrastructure. During the "13th Five-Year Plan" period, the party committee and the government of the town combined with the situation of the town to insist the development idea of "ecology first, livelihood oriented, urbanize active the town, agriculture stabilize the town, tourism thriving the town, culture settle the town and harmony maintain the town", and fight three decisive battles of preventing major risks, taking precise measures to eliminate poverty and controlling pollution, and make efforts to have breakthroughs in poverty eliminate, whole region tourism, ecology construction, rural revitalization, strengthening weak points in social programs as well as pilot and demonstration reforms, to promote the continuous and healthy development of whole town's economic society, and dedicated to construct "Humanity Shaxi, Ecology Shaxi and Intelligent Shaxi". In the future, Shaxi Town will further free the minds, seize opportunities, concentrate strengths, develop innovation, promote implementation, to lock on the construction standard of "Chinese First-class Ancient Town" and "International Level Tourism Scenery", draw sights on the developing goal of "Greater Shaxi", to put effort in building Shaxi into a tourism leisure ecological cultural town with unique characters.

大事记

2001 年 9 月，沙溪撤乡设镇。

2001年10月11日，沙溪镇寺登街区域被世界纪念性建筑遗产基金会（WMF）列入“2002年值得关注的101个世界濒危建筑遗产名录”。

2002年1月24日，沙溪镇被列为云南省历史文化名镇。

2003年，沙溪复兴工程获世界纪念性建筑基金会杰出成就奖。

2003年5月20日，沙溪寺登街区域被联合国教科文组织指定为“世界遗产、遗址脱贫的可持续实践项目框架”内的示范案例。

2004年11月28日，由大理州人民政府主办的沙溪复兴工程第一期庆典活动在寺登街举行。

2005年9月，沙溪复兴工程获联合国教科文组织“亚太地区文化遗产保护杰出贡献奖”。

2005年，沙溪镇被列入全省首批开发旅游小镇。

2006年，沙溪复兴工程获美国《休闲和旅游》杂志“2006年全球佳境奖”。

2007年，沙溪镇被命名为中国历史文化名镇。

2008年，沙溪镇被命名为云南旅游名镇。

2009年8月，沙溪镇白族传统文化保护区被云南省人民政府公布为第二批省级民族传统文化生态保护区。

2010年，寺登村被中国村社发展促进会授予“108个中国村庄名片”之一，寺登村兴教寺被列入“10个中国乡村文化遗产地标村庄名录”。

2011年，沙溪镇被云南省人民政府列入全省60个特色旅游小镇。

2011年8月，瑞士苏黎世联邦理工学院与剑川县人民政府签署《气候变化与对抗合作谅解备忘录》，在沙溪镇城隍庙片区启动实施沙溪低碳社区建设项目。

2012年，石宝山—沙溪古镇被评定为国家AAAA级旅游景区。

2014年，沙溪镇被列为全国小城镇建设试点镇。

2015年8月，沙溪镇被列为国家级建制镇示范试点镇。

2015年，中瑞双方启动第五期中瑞合作项目，进一步拓展合作方式和合作领域。

2016年11月，沙溪复兴工程获2016年中国人居环境范例奖。

2016年12月，沙溪镇启动国家第三批新型城镇化综合试点工作。

2017年6月，沙溪镇被列入全省创建全国一流特色小镇名单。

2017年7月，沙溪镇启动省级生态田园综合体试点项目。

2017年8月，沙溪古镇获得首届云南文旅融合示范景区提名奖。

2017年，沙溪镇被住房和城乡建设部列为第二批全国特色小镇。

2018年，沙溪古镇被列为全省15个优秀特色小镇之一。

2018年，沙溪镇寺登村被授予“2018年度中国美丽乡村百佳范例”称号。

2019年，沙溪镇寺登村被云南省农村人居环境整治工作领导小组评为“2019年度省级美丽村庄”。

2020年5月，沙溪镇、寺登村分别被云南省文化和旅游厅认定为云南省旅游名镇、名村。

2020年，沙溪复兴工程第五期项目作为云南省第一家入围项目被省住房和城乡建设厅推荐参加2019年度迪拜国际可持续发展最佳范例奖评选。

2020年11月，沙溪镇被中国旅游协会评为全国11个最美小镇之一。

2021年3月，沙溪镇被云南省政府命名为“云南省特色小镇”。

Chronicles

In September 2001, Shaxi became a town instead of village.

On October 11, 2001, the Sideng Street Area of Shaxi Town was listed by the World Monuments Fund (WMF) in the "World Monuments Watch List of 101 Most Endangered Sites in 2002".

On January 24, 2002, Shaxi Town was rated as a famous historical and cultural town of Yunnan Province.

In 2003, the Shaxi Rehabilitation Project was awarded for the outstanding achievement by the World Monuments Fund.

On May 20, 2003, Sideng Street area of Shaxi was appointed by the UNESCO as Pilot Case Study within the framework of the UNESCO Project "Sustainable Management of World Heriatge Sites for Poverty Reduction".

On November 28, 2004, the ceremony of the first stage of the Shaxi Rehabilitation Project was held on Sideng Street sponsored by the government of Dali.

In September 2005, the Shaxi Rehabilitation Project was awarded by UNESCO for "Award of Distinction, Asia-Pacific Heritage Awards for Cultural Heritage Conservation".

In 2005, Shaxi Town was listed as the first batch of "Developing Tourism Small Town" among the whole province.

In 2006, the Shaxi Rehabilitation Project was awarded for the "Global Vision Award 2006" by the "Travel+Leisure" magazine from America.

In 2007, Shaxi Town was named as Famous Chinese Historical Culture Town.

In 2008, Shaxi Town was named as Yunnan Famous Travelling Town.

In August of 2009, the Bai Nationality's traditional culture reserve of Shaxi Town was announced by the Yunnan Provincial Government as the second patch of Provincial Nationality Traditional Culture Ecological Protection Zone.

In 2010, Sideng Street was awarded by China Association for the Promotion of Village Community Development as one of the "108 Chinese Villages Visiting Cards", the Xingjiao Temple in Sideng Street was listed in the "List of 10 Landmark Villages of Chinese Rural Cultural Heritage".

In 2011, Shaxi Town was rated among the "60 Specialty Small Travelling Towns Among the Whole Province" by the Yunnan Provincial Government.

In August 2011, the government of Jianchuan County signed a "Memorandum of Understanding for Cooperation and Dialogue on Climate Change" with the party from Switzerland and start the construction project of the Shaxi Low-carbon Neighborhood in the Town God's Temple District of Shaxi Town.

In 2012, Mount Shibao-Shaxi Ancient Town was rated as national AAAA-Level scenery spot.

In 2014, Shaxi Town was rated as a pilot town for National Small Town Construction.

In August 2015, Shaxi Town was rated as National Demonstration Pilot Town.

In 2015, China and Switzerland started the fifth stage of China-Switzerland Cooperation Project, to further widen the cooperation manner and field.

In November of 2016, the Shaxi Rehabilitation Project won the China Habitat Environment Example Prize for 2016.

In December 2016, Shaxi Town started the work for the third batch of National Comprehensive Pilot for New Urbanization.

In June 2017, Shaxi Town was listed on the list of "National First-Class Specialty Small Town Construction" among whole province.

In July 2017, Shaxi Town started the Provincial Ecological Pastoral Complex Pilot Project.

In August 2017, Shaxi Ancient Town won the first Yunnan Cultural and Tourism Integration Demonstration Scenic Spot Nomination Award.

In 2017, Shaxi Town was rated as the second batch of National Specialty Small Town by the Ministry of Housing and Urban-Rural Development.

In 2018, Shaxi Ancient Town was listed as one of the 15 excellent Specialty Small Town among whole province.

In 2018, the Sideng Village from Shaxi Town was awarded the name of "Top 100 Examples of Beautiful Villages in China of 2018".

In 2019, the Sideng Village from Shaxi Town was rated as "Provincial Beautiful Village of 2019" by the Rural Human Settlement Environmental Remediation Working Leading Group of Yunnan Province.

In May 2020, Shaxi Town and Sideng Village was recognized as famous travelling town and village respectively by Department of Culture and Tourism of Yunnan Province.

In 2020, as the first shortlisted project from Yunnan Province, the fifth phase of the Shaxi Rehabilitation Project was recommended by the Provincial Ministry of Housing and Urban-Rural Development to attend the selection of the Best Example of Dubai International Sustainability Award in 2019.

In November of 2020, Shaxi Town was rated as one of the 11th most Beautiful National Small Town by the China Tourism Association.

In March of 2021, Shaxi Town was named by the Yunnan Provincial Government as the "Specialty Small Town of Yunnan Province".

第一章

古镇概览

Chapter 1
Ancient Town Overview

美丽的沙溪坝子 Beautiful Shaxi Basin

第一节 基本镇情

沙溪古称“沙腿”，最早见于大理国时期的《金鸡栖山石刻造像题铭》，到明代后期才称为“沙溪”，白族语言称“哨取”，今为沙溪镇。

沙溪镇位于剑川县西南部，距县城32千米，东与洱源县交界，西北与该县弥沙、羊岑、甸南三乡镇为邻，省道平甸公路纵贯沙溪坝区。

沙溪镇集坝区和山区为一体，面积287平方千米，坝区面积26平方千米，耕地面积36616亩。平均海拔2100米，年平均气温12.3℃，年平均降水量790毫米。

截至2020年底，全镇辖14个村民委员会，49个自然村，总户数5753户，人口23253人，居住有白族、汉族、彝族、傈僳族、纳西族等，其中白族人口占84%。

全镇经济以农业为主，农业以粮食种植为主，畜牧业在其中占较大比重，经济作物有油

菜、烤烟、地参等。沙溪是剑川主要产粮区之一，被誉为县内“鱼米之乡”“剑川粮仓”，主要农作物有水稻、玉米、小麦、蚕豆等。水利工程有长乐水库、石龙水库、钟山水库。土特产有地参、细鳞鱼、高原冷水鱼花鱼、松茸、牛肝菌、芸豆、梅子等。

沙溪境内名胜古迹众多，有全国重点文物保护单位石钟山石窟、兴教寺，世界纪念性建筑遗产、被誉为“茶马古道上唯一幸存的古集市”的寺登街。沙溪镇被命名为中国历史文化名镇、云南旅游名镇，“石宝山—沙溪古镇”获得国家AAAA级旅游景区称号。

沙溪的历史可追溯到2400多年前的春秋战国时期，是云南青铜文化的发源地之一，是白族本土文化、中原文化和西藏文化交会区域。沙溪有丰富的民俗文化，石宝山歌会有“千年赶一会、一会赶千年”的美誉，与“白曲”一道列入国家非物质文化遗产保护名录。沙溪的文化遗产丰富，传承方式主要依靠口述、文字记录、民间活动以及开展培训学习等。

沙溪镇人民政府引导成立沙溪民间文化传习所，发动当地居民和外地游客积极参与，许多当地非遗传人、民间艺人志愿充当传习所教员、宣传员、监督员，通过居民游客互动，让游客真实体验白族生活方式，使双方对沙溪民俗宗教、传统工艺有更深了解，打造一种深度休闲旅游的消费模式，带动当地旅游经济发展，传承非遗文化精髓，在传承民俗文化的同时使民众真正获得参与的实惠。

2004年，寺登街已完成基础设施建设。2015年以后，沙溪镇积极完善基础设施建设，主要完成道路硬化、污水处理项目、旅游道路建设、东寨门片区景观改造以及沙溪镇入口段生态廊道建设绿化，建成垃圾磁化热解站2个，完成改扩建供水管网等项目，完善全镇基础设施，改善群众生产生活条件。

通过近年的不断努力，沙溪镇基本合理配置了城乡教育、医疗、卫生、文化等公共资源，加快建成政府主导、覆盖全镇、可持续发展的基本公共服务体系。正在建设综合信息体系，可实现无线网络全覆盖、远程医疗、远程教育、电子商务、智慧安防、智慧旅游等。

2007 年，沙溪镇被命名为中国历史文化名镇
In 2007, Shaxi Town was Named as One of the Historic Towns of China

沙溪镇坚持以高原特色生态农业为基础、乡村文化体验旅游为主导，逐步形成镇区和镇域协同发展的多元化融合的产业格局，休闲旅游产业优势逐步显现。地参、泡核桃、民族手工艺等优势产业基础进一步夯实，反季蔬菜、中药材、油牡丹、中蜂养殖等潜在产业类型得到发展。沙溪镇初步形成特色化、差异化的产业发展路子。

沙溪镇紧紧围绕“产业+旅游”的发展思路，以人文沙溪、生态沙溪和智慧沙溪的发展理念，积极开展工作，带动全镇的经济发展、社会就业、产业发展、城镇化建设等。

为更好地保护和利用沙溪古镇的丰富资源，沙溪镇不断建立健全法规制度，针对核心寺登街区域成立沙溪寺登街景区管理委员会，负责古镇保护利用和建设管理。

沙溪镇按照政府引导、企业主体、社会参与、市场运作的经济发展模式推动镇域经济的良性可持续发展，努力形成全域发展的格局，沙溪的发展优势越来越凸显。

2020年，全镇经济总体平稳发展，一般公共预算收入完成10204.59万元，一般公共预算支出完成17818.13万元。农村常住居民人均可支配收入达10686.72元，农村经济持续发展，产业结构更趋合理，粮食总产量达1297.9万千克；烤烟产量达106.5万千克，烟农收入3727.5万元；畜牧业产值达15267万元；玉米制种、地参、食用玫瑰、中药材等高原特色农业培植日趋产业化规模化。第三产业提质增效，旅游资源保护、开发利用、改革创新步伐加快，全镇接待旅游人数达108.9万人次，实现旅游社会总收入13.1亿元。

Section 1　The Town's Basic Condition

The ancient name for Shaxi is "Shatui", was firstly seen in the "Golden Rooster Habitat Mountain Stone Sculpture Inscription" during the Dali Nation period and was called as "Shaxi" in the late of Ming Dynasty. The language of Bai Nationality calls it "Shaoqu", which now being the Shaxi Town.

Shaxi Town is located in the southwest of Jianchuan County and is 32 kilometers away from the county. It is bordered on the east by Eryuan County, and to the northwest it has a common border with Misha Village, Yangcen Village and Diannan Village. The provincial road—Pingdian Road passes through the basin area of Shaxi.

Shaxi Town set the basin area and mountain area as a whole, with the whole area of 288 square kilometers, the basin area has 26 square kilometers, with a total farming area of 36616 mu. The average altitude is 2100 meters, average annual temperature is 12.3°C, and the average annual precipitation is 790 mm.

By the end of 2020, the town has 14 villager committees within 49 natural villages. The total number of households is 7450, with a population of 24287. Within the town lives Bai, Han, Yi, Lisu, Naxi and other nationalities, among which the Bai Nationality accounts for 84% of population.

The town's economy is based on agriculture, and the agriculture is based on grain cultivation. Among which, livestock industry accounts for a large proportion. The economic crops include rape, cured tobacco leaves, ground ginseng etc. Shaxi is the main crops production area of Jianchuan, and is named as "Land of Fish and Rice", "The Granary

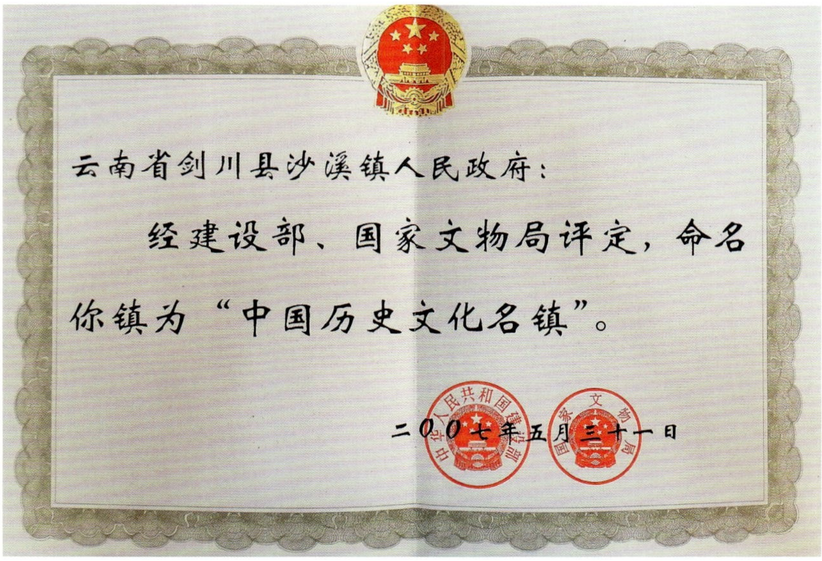

2007 年，沙溪镇被命名为中国历史文化名镇
In 2007, Shaxi Town was Named as One of the Historic Towns of China

of Jianchuan", the main crops are rice, corn, wheat, broad bean etc. Hydraulic Engineering Project includes Changle Reservoir, Shilong Reservoir, and Zhongshan Reservoir. Local special products have ground ginseng, lenok, plateau cold water fish-percocypris regani, matsutake, boletus, kidney bean, plums etc.

There are lots of scenic spots and historical sites within Shaxi border, including Shizhong Mountain Grottoes, Xingjiao Temple, which are Major National-level Protected Historical and Cultural Sites, and also Sideng Street as World Momumental Architectural Heritage, which was named as the "Only Ancient Market Survived on the Historic Tea and Horse Caravan Trail". The Shaxi Town is named as "Famous Chinese Town of History and Culture" and "Famous Yunnan Tourism Town". The "Mount Shibao-Shaxi Ancient Town" won the title of National AAAA-Level Tourist Attraction.

寺登街古戏台 Ancient Opera Stage on Sideng Street

The history of Shalxi can be traced back to the Spring and Autumn Period and the period of Warring States more than 2400 years ago, it is one of the birthplaces of Yunnan bronze culture and also an area where Bai Nationality culture, Central Plains culture and Xizang culture meet. Shaxi is rich in folk culture, the Mount Shibao Singing Party has a good reputation of "One Party Every One Thousand Years and One Party Match up to a Thousand Years" and has been listed in the National Intangible Cultural Heritage Protection List together with the "Bai Qu". Shaxi is rich in cultural heritage, which mainly relies on oral and written records, civil activities, training and learning etc.

The People's Government of Shaxi Town guides the establishment of Shaxi Civil Culture Spreading Center and encourages the active participation of residents from local area as well as tourists from other places. Many local inheritors of intangible cultural heritage and civil artists volunteer as teachers, propagandists and supervisors of the Culture Spreading Center. Through the interaction between residents and tourists, tourists can truly experience the lifestyle of Bai Nationality, so that both sides can have a deeper understanding of Shaxi civil customs, religions and traditional crafts, so as to create a deep consumption mode of leisure tourism, and also driving the development of local tourism economy and inherit the essence of intangible cultural heritage culture. To make people actually gain the benefits of participation in a real sence while inheriting civil Cultures.

In 2004, Sideng Street has finished the construction of infrastructure. After 2015, Shaxi Town start to actively perfect the infrastructure construction, and has basically finished the road hardening, sewage treatment project, tourism road construction, east gate area landscape reconstruction and the greening construction of the Shaxi Town entrance ecological corridor. Meanwhile, two waste magnetization and pyrolysis stations has been built, water supply pipe network has been expanded, the whole town's infrastructure has also been finalized, which all help improves the people's production and living conditions.

Through recent years' continuous efforts, Shaxi Town has basically allocated the public resources such as urban and rural education, medical care and culture resources, and accelerate the foundation of a basic public service system led by the government, while covering the whole town and developing sustainably. Currently, a comprehensive information system is being built to achieve wireless networks full coverage, telemedicine, distance education, e-commerce, smart security, smart tourism etc.

Base on the plateau characteristic ecological agriculture and take cultural experience tourism as leading position, Shaxi Town gradually forming a diversified and integrated industrial pattern of coordinated development of town area and town region, the advantages of leisure tourism industry has gradually been showed off. Competitive industrial bases such as ground ginseng, Juglans Sigillata and ethnic handicrafts have been further consolidated, and potential industries such as off-season vegetables, Traditional Chinese Herbal Medicine, oil peony and Chinese bee breeding have been developed. Shaxi Town has initially formed a characteristic and differentiated industrial developing path.

Centering on the development idea of "Industry+Tourism" and with the development theory of "Humanity Shaxi, Ecology Shaxi and Intelligent Shaxi", Shaxi Town has been actively implementing, to drive the economy development, society employment, industry development and urbanization construction of the whole town.

In order the further protect and utilize the abundant resource of the ancient town, Shaxi Town has been constantly establishing and improving laws and regulations. In regards of the core area of Sideng Street, Shaxi Town Managing Committee for Sideng Street Scenic Spot has been set up to be responsible for the construction management of Ancient Town's protection and utilization.

According to the economy developing mode of "Government Guidance, Enterprise Dominant, Society Participate, and Market Operate", Shaxi Town has driven a positive sustainable development of town region's economy and strives to form a whole-region development pattern. The developing advantages of Shaxi has been more and more prominent.

In 2020, the town's economy development is generally being stable, the general public budget revenue completed 102.0459 million RMB, the general public budget expenditure completed 178.1813 million RMB; The investment in fixed assets reached 684 million RMB. The per capita disposable income for permanent rural residents reached 10,686.72 RMB, the rural economy is developing sustainably, and the industry structure is more rational. The total grain output reached 12.979 million kg, the output of cured tobacco reached 1.065 million kg, the income of tobacco growers reached 37.275 million RMB, the output value of livestock reached 152.67 million RMB. The agricultural cultivation with characteristics of the plateau, such as corn seed production, ground ginseng, edible rose and Chinese Herbal Medicine, is increasingly industrialized and large-scale. The tertiary industry improved its quality and efficiency, and the protection, development and utilization, as well as reform and innovation of tourism resources were accelerated. The number of tourists received in the town reached 1.089 million, and the total income of tourism reached 1.31 billion RMB.

鸟瞰古镇　Bird View of the Ancient Town

第二节　区位优势

沙溪镇位于剑川县西南部，距剑川县城32千米，地处世界自然遗产金沙江、澜沧江、怒江三江并流自然保护区域东南部，位于大理、丽江、香格里拉旅游区之间，地处北纬26°11′~26°19′，东经99°45′~99°58′。东与洱源县交界，西北与剑川县弥沙、羊岑、甸南三乡镇为邻，紧邻国家级风景区石宝山。沙溪坝四面环山，澜沧江水系黑潓江由北至南纵贯全坝。沙溪镇镇政府驻地寺登街位于沙溪坝子中部，为全镇的政治、经济、文化、商业服务和交通中心。平甸公路由漾濞县平坡镇经洱源的炼铁乡、乔后镇，穿过沙溪镇全境后至剑川县甸南镇与214国道相连接。镇区有多条乡道联系镇域内各村民委员会及部分自然村。

2400多年前，沙溪就形成了以黑潓江为中心的青铜冶炼制作基地，沙溪先人在那时就拥有了较高的青铜冶炼技术，成为云南青铜文化的发源地之一。鳌峰山古墓葬群和沙溪东面华丛山铜矿遗址遗留至今。

唐宋时期，南诏、大理国等民族政权相继在西南地区建立，沙溪处古滇藏道（今214国道），北上可至丽江、迪庆，进入西藏；南经大理、保山、德宏可至缅甸、印度。再加上南诏、大理国时期开凿的石钟山石窟，沙溪在茶马古道上成为贸易集散地，南诏、大理国时期为佛教文化活动中心，并逐步发展成为经贸发达、文化繁荣的古镇。

唐代以后，位于沙溪西部的弥沙开始开采井盐，沙溪是离弥沙盐井最近的茶马古道集市，一跃成为茶马古道上的盐都，成为西藏、滇西北地区食盐供给的重要集散地。沙溪成为茶马古道上农业、工业、商业、交通运输业等经济最发达的地区之一。

元代以后，由于今邓川坝中道路的开通，

加上建置和疆域的变迁，沙溪在滇西北政治、经济、军事、文化中心的重要地位发生了变化，但茶马古道沿用至今。时至今日，通往马坪关、石宝山的两条古道依然保存完好，古道上面还能清晰地看到马帮行走时马蹄踩出的印记。

寺登街是镇政府所在地，位于沙溪坝中部，是全镇的交通枢纽，与镇域其他村民委员会、剑川县城和周边乡镇都有交通联系，具备生态旅游发展和城镇整体提升的区位交通条件。滇川藏大香格里拉生态旅游区的快速发展，为丽江—剑川—鹤庆成为滇西北旅游中一个重要的核心三角

沙溪坝子一角 A Glimpse of the Shaxi Basin

区带来新机遇。随着大丽高速公路的建成通车，丽江机场成为沙溪镇与外界联系的新兴交通通道，也为沙溪建设休闲度假型生态旅游小镇带来更好的发展机遇。

2019年10月，鹤剑兰高速沙溪支线项目正式启动。项目全长19.8千米，按双向四车道高速公路标准建设，设计速度80千米/时，桥涵设计荷载等级为公路一级。截至2020年底，累计完成投资6.02亿元，开挖隧道7264.7千米，实施路基挖方180万立方米、桥梁桩基240根，全面完成房屋等拆迁工作。作为鹤剑兰高速的重要组成部分、滇西北黄金旅游经济命脉之一，项目建成后将终结沙溪交通滞后的历史，拉近沙溪与周边景点景区的距离，引领沙溪这个中国历史文化名镇进入高速发展时代。

马帮行走的年代，沙溪是滇藏茶马古道上的一个重要驿站，是马帮人心中温暖的港湾。现在的沙溪古镇是大理、丽江和香格里拉黄金旅游带上的一个重要节点，远离城市喧嚣，是游客心中优美的家园。

沙溪交通网　Shaxi Transportation Network

Section 2 Geographical Advantages

Shaxi Town is located in the southwest of Jianchuan County and is 32 kilometers away from the county, it is located in the southeast of the world natural heritage Jinsha River, Lancang River and Nu River parallel flowing nature reserve area, and is within Dali, Lijiang and Shangri-La tourist area, the north latitude is between 26°11′~26°19′ and the east longitude is between 99°45′~99°58′. It is bordered on the east by Eryuan County, and to the northwest it has a common border with Misha Village, Yangcen Village and Diannan Village of Jianchuan County and close to the National Scenic Spot-Mount Shibao. The Shaxi Basin is surrounded with mountains, and the Heisui River from the Lancang River System runs through the whole basin area from north to south. Shaxi Town's government's location—Sideng Street is in the middle area of Shaxi Basin area, it is the town's political, economic, cultural, commercial services and transportation center. The Pingdian Road started from the Pingpo Town of Yangbi County runs through the Liantie Village and Qiaohou Town of Eryuan County and connected to the No.214 National Road in Diannan Town of Jianchuan County after runs through the whole Shaxi Town. There are a number of township roads connecting each villager committees and part of the natural villages within the town territory.

More than 2400 years ago, Shaxi has formed a bronze smelting production base centered on Heihui River. Shaxi ancestors had relatively high bronze smelting technology at that time, becoming one of the cradles of bronze culture in Yunnan. The Aofeng Mountain Ancient Tomb Group and the Huacong Mountain copper mine site east of Shaxi remain to now.

During the Tang and Song dynasties, Nanzhao and Dali emerged in southwest China. Shaxi was located on the ancient Yunnan-Xizang Road (Now National Road 214), and reached Lijiang and Diqing in the north, and entered the Xizang area. South through Dali, Baoshan, Dehong to Myanmar, India's important sites. Plus the Shizhong Mountain Grottoes excavated in the period of Nanzhao and Dali, Shaxi has become a trade distribution center on the Historic Tea and Horse Caravan Trail and the Center of Buddhist cultural activities in the period of Nanzhao and Dali, and gradually become an Ancient Town with developed economy and trade as well as prosperous culture.

After the Tang Dynasty, well salt began to be

美丽的沙溪坝子 Beautiful Shaxi Basin

mined in Misha in the west of Shaxi. Shaxi was the nearest market of the Historic Tea and Horse Caravan Trail to Misha Salt Well so it became the salt capital of the Historic Tea and Horse Caravan Trail, and an important distribution center for salt supply in Xizang and northwest of Yunnan. Shaxi has become one of the most economically developed areas of agriculture, industry, commerce and transportation on the Historic Tea and Horse Caravan Trail.

After the Yuan Dynasty, due to the opening of the Bazhong Road in Dengchuan Basin, as well as the changes of construction and territory, Shaxi's important position in the political, economic, military and cultural center of northwest Yunnan has changed, but the Historic Tea and Horse Caravan Trail is still in use till today. Even today, the two ancient roads leading to Maping Pass and Mount Shibao are well preserved, and the marks made by horse caravans can be clearly seen on the ancient roads.

Being the location of the town government, Sideng Street is in the middle of Shaxi Basin, it is the transportation junction of the town. It is connected with other Villagers' committees in the town, Jianchuan County and surrounding towns, and has the location and transportation conditions for the development of ecological tourism and the overall improvement of the town. The rapid development of Yunnan-Sichuan-Xizang Shangri-La Eco-tourism Area has brought new opportunities for Lijiang-Jianchuan-Heqing to become an important core triangle area in northwest Yunnan tourism. With the completion and opening to traffic of Dali Expressway, Lijiang Airport has become a new traffic channel for Shaxi Town to connect with the outside world, and it also brings better development opportunities for Shaxi to build a leisure and holiday-oriented ecological tourism town.

In October 2019, the Hejianlan Expressway Shaxi Branch Project was officially launched. The total length of the project is 19.8 km, according to the standard construction of two-way four-lane expressway, the design speed is 80 km/h, and the design load grade of the bridge and culvert is primary highway level. Until the end of 2020, it has finished an investment of 602 million RMB, dug in 7264.7 kilometers of tunnel, dug 1.8 million cubic meters of roadbed, piled 240 bridge foundations, and completely finished the housing demolished. As an important composition of Hejianlan Expressway and one of the gold tourisms economic lifeline in northwest Yunnan, this project, will put an end to the history of traffic lag in Shaxi when it is completed, shorten the distance between Shaxi and surrounding scenic spots, and lead Shaxi, a famous historical and cultural town in China, into the era of rapid development.

During the timing when horse caravans was travelling, Shaxi was an important station on the Yunnan-Xizang Historic Tea and Horse Caravan Trail, and a warm harbor in the heart of the caravans. Nowadays, Shaxi Ancient Town is an important junction on the golden tourism belt of Dali, Lijiang and Shangri-La. It is far away from the hustle and bustle of the city, and also a beautiful home in the heart of tourists.

丛林中的古道 Ancient Path in the Jungle

第三节　优质发展

沙溪镇辖寺登、东南、华龙、北龙、四联、甸头、沙坪、石龙、长乐、鳌凤、灯塔、溪南、红星、联合14个行政村。镇政府驻寺登街。

根据沙溪镇镇域地理位置、自然条件、地形地势、生产力布局特点、各村委会经济发展现状和经济发展潜力，《剑川县沙溪镇总体规划（2012—2030）》以圈层的模式将沙溪镇规划为三个经济发展区。

1.内圈层——镇区经济区

以沙溪镇区为中心，包括下科自然村、江乐禾自然村、中登自然村。依托沙溪镇区的建设带动经济发展，为沙溪镇经济较好地区，其基础服务设施较为完善，交通条件便利，集中了镇域内大部分的餐饮业、休闲娱乐、商贸等服务业，经济收入占全镇经济收入的60%以上。

2.中圈层——坝区经济区

以甸头、沙坪、四联、北龙、华龙、东南（除江乐禾村）、长乐、鳌凤（除中登村）、灯塔、溪南、红星等镇区外围坝区内行政村为主的区域，结合坝区农业发展，以粮食生产、烤烟、畜牧及核桃、板栗经济林果、特色农业和农副产品食品加工为主的经济区。

3.外圈层——半山区、山区经济区

坝区外以石龙、联合行政村为主的半山区和山区地区，以发展马铃薯、芸豆、板栗、核桃、畜牧业、粮食种植为主的一般农业经济区。

沙溪镇以农业产业化发展为主攻方向，进一步优化结构调整，基地规模不断壮大。在坝区重

华龙村传统农耕场景　Traditional Farming Scene of Hualong Village

“二牛抬杠”——传统农耕形式　"Two- cattle Carrying Pole"—Traditional Farming Form

烤烟种植　Cured Tobacco Planting

点发展高原优质粳稻、烤烟、啤大麦、乳畜、生猪等产业，半山区、山区重点发展泡核桃、肉牛（羊）、芸豆、地膜苞谷等产业，形成高海拔冷凉地区的农业产业化发展格局。

沙溪镇是中国历史文化名镇，文化底蕴深厚，古建民居众多，14个行政村中有7个传统村落。沙溪镇以打造“大滇西旅游环线上的魅力沙溪”为发展目标，以寺登村为中心辐射带动周边村庄发展乡村旅游，不断完善传统村落基础设施建设，累计投入5000多万元对寺登、四联、甸头、长乐、鳌凤、华龙、石龙等7个传统村落部分污水管网进行提升改造，结合省级特色小镇创建，对部分传统建筑进行修缮保护，活化利用空心村，挖掘传统村落文化内涵，让传统村落换新颜，着力建设美丽宜居乡村。

北龙村油菜花田　Rape Flower Field of Beilong Village

2. Middle District: Basin Area Economic Zone

This area is basically the village area outside the town and within the basin area, including Diantou Village, Shaping Village, Silian Village, Beilong Village, Hualong Village, Dongnan Village (Except Jianglehe Village), Changle Village, Aofeng Village (Except Zhongdeng Village), Dengta Village, Xinan Village, Hongxing Village. Combining with the basin area's agriculture development, this is an economic area centralized with grain production, cured tobacco, livestock, walnut, chestnut special fruit woods, special agriculture and sideline food production industry.

3. Outer District: Halfway-Hill and Mountain Area Economic Zone

Outside the basin area is the half mountain areas and mountain area, mainly be the Shilong Village and joint administrative village. Developing general agriculture economic zone centralized with potato, kidney bean, chestnut, walnut, livestock, grain production industries.

Shaxi Town takes agricultural industrialization development as main direction, with further structure adjustment optimization, the basic scale is continuously expending. Within the basin zone, the development focus on high quality japonica rice, cured tobacco, beer barley, dairy cattle, live pig industries. While within half mountain areas and mountain zone, the development focus on juglants sigillata, beef (Mutton), kidney bean, plastic film corn industries. Finally form the pattern of agricultural industrialization development in high altitude cool areas.

Shaxi Town is a famous Chinese history and culture town with a deep culture heritage and many ancient dwellings, there are 7 traditional villages within its 14 administrative villages. Making "The Charming Shaxi on the Great West Yunnan Tourism Loop" as its developing goal, Shaxi Town use Sideng Village as its center and drives those surrounding villages to develop suburban tourism, and also constantly improve the infrastructure construction for traditional villages. Shaxi Town has put in more than 50 million RMB to upgrade and rebuilt the sewage network for 7 traditional villages including Sideng, Silian, Diantou, Changle, Aofeng, Hualong, Shilong. Combining with the establishment of provincial Specialty Small Town, part of those traditional buildings was also repaired and protected. Utilizing those hollow villages, the cultural connotation of traditional villages exploring, through these improvements, the Shaxi Town gives traditional villages a new look, and strive to build a beautiful and livable countryside.

长乐村传统农耕　Traditional Farming Scene of Changle Village

第二章

生态环境

Chapter 2 Ecological Environment

第一节　自然地理

沙溪古镇东临华丛山，南接洱源县乔后镇，西靠鹅顶山和石宝山，北连剑川甸南镇，地势北高南低，是华丛山与石宝山南迤的中间平坝，东西宽4.5千米，南北长16.4千米，坝区面积26平方千米。坝子中部有一座丘陵，高出地面40米，名鳌峰山或羊子头坡。坝尾米子坪海拔1973米，为县内海拔最低点。

澜沧江水系黑潓江由北至南纵贯全坝，以白族为主的各族群众聚居的村落散居于黑潓江两岸。

黑潓江发源于剑湖，流经剑川、洱源两县（剑川境内为31千米），宽24~70米，最大流量561.8立方米/秒，最枯流量7.87立方米/秒，剑川县境内流域面积为328平方千米，有灌溉和发电之利。

沙溪四面环山，属北温带季风气候，北面层层的山岭挡住了哈巴雪山、玉龙雪山的寒流，年平均气温12.3℃。年日照时数2400小时，年降水量790毫米，无霜期215天。

华龙秋韵　Autumn Scenery of Hualong

黑溏江深秋　Late Autumn Scenery of Heihui River

Section 1 Natural and Geography

Shaxi Ancient Town, which is near to Huacong Mountain in the east, Qiaohou Town of Eryuan Country in the south, Eding Mountain and Mount Shibao in the west, and Dianan Town of Jianchuan in the north, with the terrain being high in the north and low in the south, is the central flat basin in the middle of Huacong Mountain and Mount Shibao's southern extending, whose width is 4.5km from east to west and length is 16.4km from north to south, and the area of the basin is 26km^2. There is a hill in the middle of the basin, 40m above the ground, named Aofeng Mountain or Yangzitou Slope. Miziping at the end of the basin is with 1973m elevation, which is the lowest place in the county.

The Heihui River of the Lancang River system flows through the whole basin from north to south, and the inhabitants from various nationalities, mainly Bai Nationality, live on both sides of the Heihui River.

Heihui River originates from Jianhu, flows through Jianchuan County and Eryuan County (31km in Jianchuan Field), width is 24-70m, the max. flow is 561.8m^3/s, the min. flow is 7.87m^3/s, the watershed area is 328km^2 in Jianchuan County, to use for irrigation and power generation.

Shaxi, surrounded by mountains, is north temperate monsoon climate, layers of mountains at the north block the cold current from Haba Snow Mountain and Yulong Snow Mountain, annual average temperature is 12.3°C. Annual sunshine time is 2400h, annual precipitation is 790mm, frost-free time is 215 days.

丹霞地貌景观　Landscape of Danxia Landform

沙登箐丹霞地貌　Danxia Landform of Shadengqing

第二节　自然资源

沙溪境内土壤由于受到河流泥沙的冲击，成分丰富、肥力较高，土壤类型为暗棕壤、棕壤、红棕壤、黄棕壤，水利水源充足，水热条件较好。

全镇森林覆盖率达82%，动植物资源丰富，有云南松、华山松、香樟、红豆杉、漆树等树种，有杜鹃、山茶、兰花等花卉，有松茸、牛肝菌、羊肚菌等菌类，有猕猴、野猪、锦鸡、獐子、穿山甲等动物。

Section 2　Natural Resources

Due to the river sediment, the soil in Shaxi has rich composition and high fertility, the soil types are dark brown soil, brown soil, red brown soil and yellow brown soil, the water source is sufficient and the hydrothermal condition is good.

The town's overall forest coverage rate is 82%, with rich in animal and plant resources, including Yunnan pine, Huashan pine, camphor, taxus, lacquer tree and other tree species, rhododendron, camellia, orchids and other flower species, matsutake, porcini, morchella and other fungi species, macaque, wild boar, pheasant, river deer, pangolin and other animal species.

黑潓江滋润下的“鱼米之乡” The "Land of Fish and Rice" Nourished by Heihui River

黑惠江畔棠梨花开　The Blooming Pyrus Betulaefolia by Heihui River

石宝山猕猴（一） The Macaque from Mount Shibao (1)

石宝山猕猴（二） The Macaque from Mount Shibao (2)

马醉木 The Pieris Japonica D. Don

大树杜鹃花 The Tree Rhododendron

兰花 The Orchids

山玉兰花 The Mountain Magnolia

第三章

民族 宗教

Chapter 3
Nationality and Religion

剑川传统白族服饰——衣子比甲　Traditional Jianchuan Bai Nationality Dress—Yizi Vest

第一节　多民族共处

沙溪地处金沙江、澜沧江、怒江三江并流世界自然遗产区老君山片区东南端，黑潓江由北至南纵贯全坝，山、水、田、村自然融合，分布有序，形成“山环水绕，世外乡居”的林盘平坝。村镇之间，生态水系与田野绿化相互交融；村屋前后，空地皆为菜地田园，与黑潓江蜿蜒相伴。沙溪居住有白族、汉族、彝族、傈僳族等世居民族，其中白族人口占84%。彝族群众主要分布在华丛山、长乐后山；傈僳族聚居于北龙村，住在甸头山上；汉族则集中于红星村，东南伙山一、二社。沙溪的白族除保留了自身的民族语言、生活习俗外，主要吸收了汉族的文化和习俗。至今，白族语言、风俗习惯中还保留着中原已失传的古汉语借词和汉族风俗习惯，这些丰富了白族的文化生活内容。随着各种文化传播到沙溪，大量推动社会前进的各类生产技术、技艺进入境内，促进了沙溪刺绣、木雕等技艺发展，并发展成为独树一帜的地方民族工艺。在与白族共同生产生活的过程中，其他少数民族由于社会交际所需，既保留了各自的民族语言和习俗，又大量学习使用白族语言和习俗。长期以来，沙溪镇境内各世居民族互相依存、携手共进、和睦相处，以博大的胸怀气魄、精深的聪明才智、顽强的拼搏精神，创造了灿烂的历史文化，共同推动沙溪经济发展和社会进步，共同奏响了民族大团结的华美乐章，共同绘就了一幅民族团结、社会和谐的美好画卷。

沙溪米子坪白族服饰——山花服　Miziping Bai Nationality Dress of Shaxi—Mountain Flower Dress

Section 1 Multi-ethnic Coexistence

Shaxi is located at Jinsha River, Lancang River and Nu River parallel flow area, southeast of the World Natural Heritage area Laojun Mountain, the Heihui River flows through the whole basin from north to south, with mountains, rivers, fields and villages naturally merged and orderly distributed, forming a flat basin with "Mountains and Rivers Surrounding and Real Villeggiatura". Among the villages and towns, Ecological water system and field greening intermingle; beside the rooms of villagers, fields are filled with crops, accompanying the winding Heihui River. The inhabitants live in Shaxi include Bai, Han, Yi, Lisu and other nationalities, among these, Bai Nationality takes 84% of the population. The Yi inhabitants mainly live at Huacong Mountain and Changle Back Mountain; Lisu people gather at Beilong Village, live at Diantou Mountain; while Han people gather at Hongxin Village and Southeast Huoshan community

1 and 2. For the Bai Nationality inhabitants live in Shaxi, they not only retain their own language and customs, and also absorb the culture and customs of Han Nationality. Till now, the language and customs of Bai Nationality still retain the central plain lost ancient Chinese loanwords and customs of Han Nationality, which enrich the cultural life of the Bai Nationality. With various culture being spread to Shaxi, a large amount of production technology and skills which put society moving forward enter the territory, promoting the development of embroidery and wood carving at Shaxi, and developed into unique local craft. During the process of living together with Bai Nationality people, the other minority nationalities not only retain their own language and customs, but also learn to use Bai Nationality's language and customs, due to the social communication needs. In long period, the people from each nationality in Shaxi Town depend on each other, improve together, be happy together, with broad mind, profound intelligence and tenacious fighting spirit, creating splendid history and culture, promoting the development of Shaxi's economic development and social progress together, playing a beautify music chapter of great national unity together, painting a glorious scroll of national unity and social harmony together.

华龙村华丛山彝族群众　Yi People at Hualong Village Huacong Mountain

石龙霸王鞭　The Bawang's Whip at Shilong

沙溪傈僳族服饰　Lisu Nationality Dress of Shaxi

沙溪的彝族群众　Yi People at Shaxi

沙溪彝族服饰　Yi Nationality Dress of Shaxi

兴教寺大门　The Gate of Xingjiao Temple

第二节　宗教信仰多元化

沙溪处于大理、丽江之间，是滇藏茶马古道上一个重要集市，再加上南诏、大理国石窟的开凿，沙溪在茶马古道上成为贸易集散地、南诏大理国佛教文化传统活动地，是一个集商贸与佛教文化为一体的古镇。

佛教文化在大理地区传播过程中，为更好地获得民众的支持，逐渐形成与民间信仰相融合的世俗化过程。佛教密宗阿吒力文化在白族社会生活中的普及使白族民间信仰中原有的非佛教文化因素逐渐被佛教文化活动所取代。此后，外来密宗文化与白族文化长期相融，形成自成体系的白族阿吒力文化。

除此，沙溪最主要的信仰是本主崇拜。“本主”指本境福主，是一村一寨或一个区域的保护神。白族本主崇拜思想与其先民的原始宗教观念有很深的渊源，因此可视为一种祖先崇拜，从天地、日月、星辰、山林、洪水等自然事物到历代南诏王、贤臣良将、英雄义士等，乃至佛教、道教以及儒家的一些神和圣贤都是本主崇拜的对象。早期本主崇拜经历南诏大理国及之后的长时间发展，在广泛吸收佛、道、儒三教的思想之后，逐渐形成如今人们看到的一个较为成熟的宗教思想。正因如此，白族本主崇拜有深厚的文化内涵并具有自己的特征。本主崇拜是一种多神崇拜，各地或各个村寨本主庙内都塑有自己的本主神。也有的几个村寨甚至几十个村寨共同信奉一个本主。

白族阿吒力文化数字化展示及应用项目　Digital Display and Application Project of Acarya Culture in Bai Nationality

沙溪本主祭祀活动　Sacrificial Activity for Local Deity at Shaxi

Section 2 Diversity of Religious Belief

Shaxi, located between Dali and Lijiang, is an important bazaar along the Yunnan-Xizang Historic Tea and Horse Caravan Trail, addition to the excavating of Nanzhao and Dali Grottoes, Shaxi becoming a trading hub and becoming a place for Nanzhao & Dali traditional buddhist culture activities, is an ancient town integrated with trade and buddhist culture.

During the spreading process, in order to gain better popular support, buddhist culture gradually forms a secularization process integrated with people's belief. The popularization of Buddhist Tantric Acarya Culture in Bai Nationality makes the non-buddhist cultural factors among Bai Nationality people being gradually replaced by buddhist cultural activities. Since then, foreign tantric culture and Bai Nationality culture going through a long-term integration, which forms self-contained Bai Nationality Acarya Culture.

In addition, Local Deity is a mainly worshiped god at Shaxi. "Local Deity", being a local blessing god, is a guardian god for each village or area. Bai Nationality people's Local Deity worship ideology has a deep connection with their primitive religious ideas of their ancestors, so it can be taken as a kind of ancestor worship, from natural objects like heaven and earth, sun and moon, stars, forests, flood to Nanzhao Kings, virtuous ministers and generals, heroes, etc., even some gods and sages of buddhism, taoism and confucianism are the objects of worship. The early Local Deity worship experienced Nanzhao Dali and its following long-time development, after the extensive absorption of buddhism, taoism and confucianism, gradually formed a more mature religious ideology which we can see now. For this reason, Bai Nationality people's Local Deity worship has profound cultural connotation and

its own characteristics. Local Deity worship is a kind of multi-deity worship, so there is own Deity being sculptured in their Local Deity Temple in each district or village. There are also situations that several or dozens of villages worship one same Local Deity.

白族佛教“妈妈会”社团　The Buddhism "Mothers' Union" in Bai Nationality

宗教信仰　Religious Belief

白族佛教社会组织“妈妈会”民间社庆活动　The Social Celebration Activities of the Buddhism "Mothers' Union" in Bai Nationality

白族阿吒力文化科仪（一） Ritual of Bai Nationality Acarya Culture (1)

白族阿吒力文化科仪（二） Ritual of Bai Nationality Acarya Culture (2)

第四章

记忆沙溪

Chapter 4
Memory of Shaxi

第一节　鳌峰山古墓群

沙溪鳌峰山古墓群位于剑川县沙溪镇寺登村南500米的鳌峰山顶。1980年10月，经云南省文物工作队发掘清理，墓地揭露面积540平方米，清理瓮棺墓34座、火葬墓91座、土坑墓217座，出土器物658件。农耕土下即为瓮棺墓和火葬墓，均用形体多变的陶瓮、陶罐作葬具，瓮棺墓均埋幼童，火葬墓均埋成人，骨骼烧成粉末，少许尚能辨认肢骨、头骨，个别用铜镯随葬。瓮棺墓、火葬墓下为土坑墓。除24座墓内的尸骨已成粉末或后期破坏不易辨认葬式外，其余当属单人葬和合葬。单人葬174座，其中仰身直肢葬144座，二次葬27座，解肢葬2座，无头葬1座。合葬19座，其中仰身直肢与侧身屈肢合葬6座，仰身直肢与殉人合葬6座，仰身直肢二人合葬3座，母

鳌峰山出土的钺范　The Tomahawk Model Unearthed from Aofeng Mountain

鳌峰山出土的铁器　The Iron Wares Unearthed from Aofeng Mountain

沙溪鳌峰山古墓葬群所在地　The Location of Shaxi Aofeng Mountain Ancient Tombs

子合葬2座，俯身直肢与殉人合葬1座，侧身断肢与殉人合葬1座。

根据出土文物鉴定，鳌峰山墓葬时代约当春秋晚期至西汉初期。经对出土文物中早期第50号墓人骨进行放射性碳素测定，为距今2420±80年；中期第19号墓人骨距今2295±75年。墓葬出土铜器数量和品种繁多，冶铸技术已相当精良。从出土的玛瑙珠、绿松石、海贝等东南亚地区产物来看，这里在当时已经是对外交流的重要通道了。

经过考古专家研究，沙溪鳌峰山墓地出土文物具有显著的土著特点，属于洱海地区青铜文化的重要源头之一。它的发现对研究洱海地区乃至云南高原的青铜文化及社会发展情况都具有重要的历史意义。

Section 1 Ancient Tombs on Aofeng Mountain

The Shaxi Aofeng Mountain Ancient Tombs are located at the peak of Aofeng Mountain, which is 500m south of Sideng Village, Shaxi Town, Jianchuan County. In October 1980, explored and cleaned by Yunnan cultural relics work team, the tombs' area is 540m², and 34 urn coffin tombs, 91 cremation tombs and 217 pit tombs were cleaned, 658 artifacts were unearthed. The urn coffin tombs and cremation tombs were just beneath the agricultural soil, and they all used multi-shaped pottery urns and pottery pots as burial wares, urn coffin tombs to bury toddlers and cremation tombs to bury adults, with bones burned into powder, a few them can still be recognized as limbs or head, several of them were buried together with bronze bracelets. The pit tombs were under the urn coffin tombs and the cremation tombs. Except 24 tombs' burial method were unrecognizable because of the bones being powder or damaged, the others were single burial and joint burial. There were 174 single burials, including 144 flat burials with straight limbs, 27 secondary burials, 2 dismembered burials and 1 burial without head. There were 19 joint burials, including 6 flat burials with straight limbs and side burials with crooked limbs, 6 flat burials with straight limbs and with buried alive body, 3 flat burials with straight limbs two-body joint burials, 2 mother and son joint burials, 1 face-down burial with straight limbs and with buried alive body, 1 side burial with broken limbs and with buried alive body.

According the identification of the unearthed artifacts, the age of Aofeng Mountain Ancient Tombs is about from late Spring and Autumn to early Western Han Dynasty. After radiocarbon

鳌峰山出土的青铜剑 The Bronze Sword Unearthed from Aofeng Mountain

鳌峰山出土的青铜器 The Bronze Ware Unearthed from Aofeng Mountain

determination carried out on the bones from No. 50 tomb in the early period, they are around 2420±80 years ago; the bones from No. 19 tomb in the middle period are around 2295±75 years ago. There are large quantity and various of the unearthed bronze wares from the tombs, with sophisticated metallurgy technology. From the unearthed agate beads, turquoise, seashells and other products from Southeast Asia, we can see this place was already a very important path for external communication.

After the study of archaeological experts, the unearthed artifacts from Shaxi Aofeng Mountain Ancient Tombs have very significant indigenous characteristics, which is one of the important origins of bronze culture in Erhai area. Its findings have very important historical meaning to study bronze culture and social development of Erhai area and even Yunnan plateau.

第二节　石钟山石窟

石宝山坐落于剑川县城西南21千米处，总面积25平方千米。石宝山山脚下就是茶马古道重镇——沙溪古镇。石宝山景区历史悠久，古迹荟萃。景区主要由石钟山石窟、宝相寺、金顶寺、海云居、石龙民族文化村组成。石钟山石窟是中国石窟艺术由敦煌开始一直往南延伸，结束在剑川石钟山的石窟艺术，是一部镶刻在石头上的云南历史。

石钟山石窟分布在方圆3平方千米的石钟寺、狮子关、沙登箐三个区域的岩壁上，是唐宋南诏、大理国时期（738—1253）的艺术瑰宝。根据云南大学、北京大学联合考古队1999年的考古调查，石钟山石窟共17窟，233躯造像。石窟内有南诏天启十一年（850）和大理国盛德四年（1179）题记，可知石钟山石窟开凿已有1000多年的历史，整个石窟开凿前后持续320多年。石窟造像不仅生动地展现了流传于大理地区的白族阿吒力文化中的佛、菩萨、明王、力士等造像，而且大胆地开凿了“阿姎白”女性生殖崇拜雕刻、南诏王室的政治生活和家庭生活图像等内容，在世界石窟艺术史上极为罕见。石窟造像造型生动，形象逼真，雕刻技巧纯熟，线条细腻流畅，且题材丰富、构思独特，具有浓郁的民族风格和鲜明的地方特色。

“北有敦煌壁画，南有剑川石窟”——剑川石钟山石窟作为云南省石窟的代表，荣登第一批全国重点文物保护单位名单，与甘肃敦煌的莫高窟、天水的麦积山石窟、山西大同的云冈石窟、河南洛阳的龙门石窟等蜚声海外的石窟齐名，当代武侠小说家金庸先生为其留下“南天瑰宝”的题字。2004年4月18日，著名作家冯骥才到石宝山考察，题词“神佛首选地，人间天堂山”，并写下《解密阿姎白》一文。

石钟寺　Shizhong Temple

狮子关　Shiziguan

凌云柱　Lingyunzhu

朝天笏　Chaotian Wat

阁罗凤出巡图　Geluofeng Patrol Picture

甘露观音　Ganlu Avalokitesvara

维摩诘“问疾品”造像　Statue of Vimalakirti Is "Asking for Diseases"

明王堂　The Ming King's Hall

金庸先生题字“南天瑰宝”　Mr. Jin Yong's Inscription "Treasure of the Southern Sky"

Section 2　Shizhong Mountain Grottoes

Mount Shibao is located at 21km southwest of Jianchuan County, its total area is 25km², and the Shaxi Ancient Town, an important town of the Historic Tea and Horse Caravan Trail is at the foot of the Mount Shibao. Mount Shibao scenery has long history and be well-known with various sites. Shizhong Mountain Grottoes, Baoxiang Temple, Jinding Temple, Haiyunju and Shilong nationality cultural village are the main parts of the scenery. Shizhong Mountain Grottoes are the grottoes art starting at Dunhuang and extending south, until ending at Shizhong Mountain in Jianchuan County, and also are history of Yunnan which are carved on stone.

Shizhong Mountain Grottoes spread over 3km² cliff of Shizhog Temple, Shiziguan and Shadengqing, are art treasures of Tang, Song, Nanzhao and Dali period (738—1253). According to the survey of Yunnan University and Peking University joint team in 1999, Shizhong Mountain Grottoes have 17 caves and 233 statues in total. In the grottoes, there are inscriptions in 11th year of Nanzhao Tianqi (850) and 4th year of Shengde Dali (1179), so we can see the excavating of Shizhong Mountain Grottoes has more than 1000 years history, the whole excavating process lasted more than 320 years. The statues in the grottoes not only display the statues of Buddha, Bodhisattva, Ming King and Hercules, which are popular in the Acharya Culture of Bai Nationality in Dali area, but also boldly excavate "Ayangbai" female reproduction worship sculpture, and Nanzhao royal family's political life and family life images, which are extremely rare in world grotto art history. The grottoes have vivid shapes and images, with skillful caving to form smooth and delicate lines, with abundant themes and unique ideas, to

大黑天王造像　The Mahakala Statue

明代岩画　The Cliff Painting of Ming Dynasty

express rich nationality style and distinctive local characteristics.

"There are Dunhuang Murals at the North, and there are Jianchuan Grottoes at the South"-Jianchuan Shizhong Mountain Grottoes, as the representative of grottoes in Yunnan Province, are listed on the first batch of Major National-level Protected Historical and Cultural Sites, are as famous as Dunhuang Mogao Grottoes in Gansu Province, Maiji Mountain Grottoes in Tianshui, Yungang Grottoes in Datong of Shanxi Province, and Longmen Grottoes in Luoyang of Henan Province. Jin Yong, a contemporary martial arts novelist, wrote the inscription "Treasure of the Southern Sky" for it. April 18, 2004, the famous writer Feng Jicai visited Mount Shibao, inscribed "The Best Place for Gods and Buddhas, the Paradise Mountain on the Earth", and wrote the article "Decryption of Ayangbai".

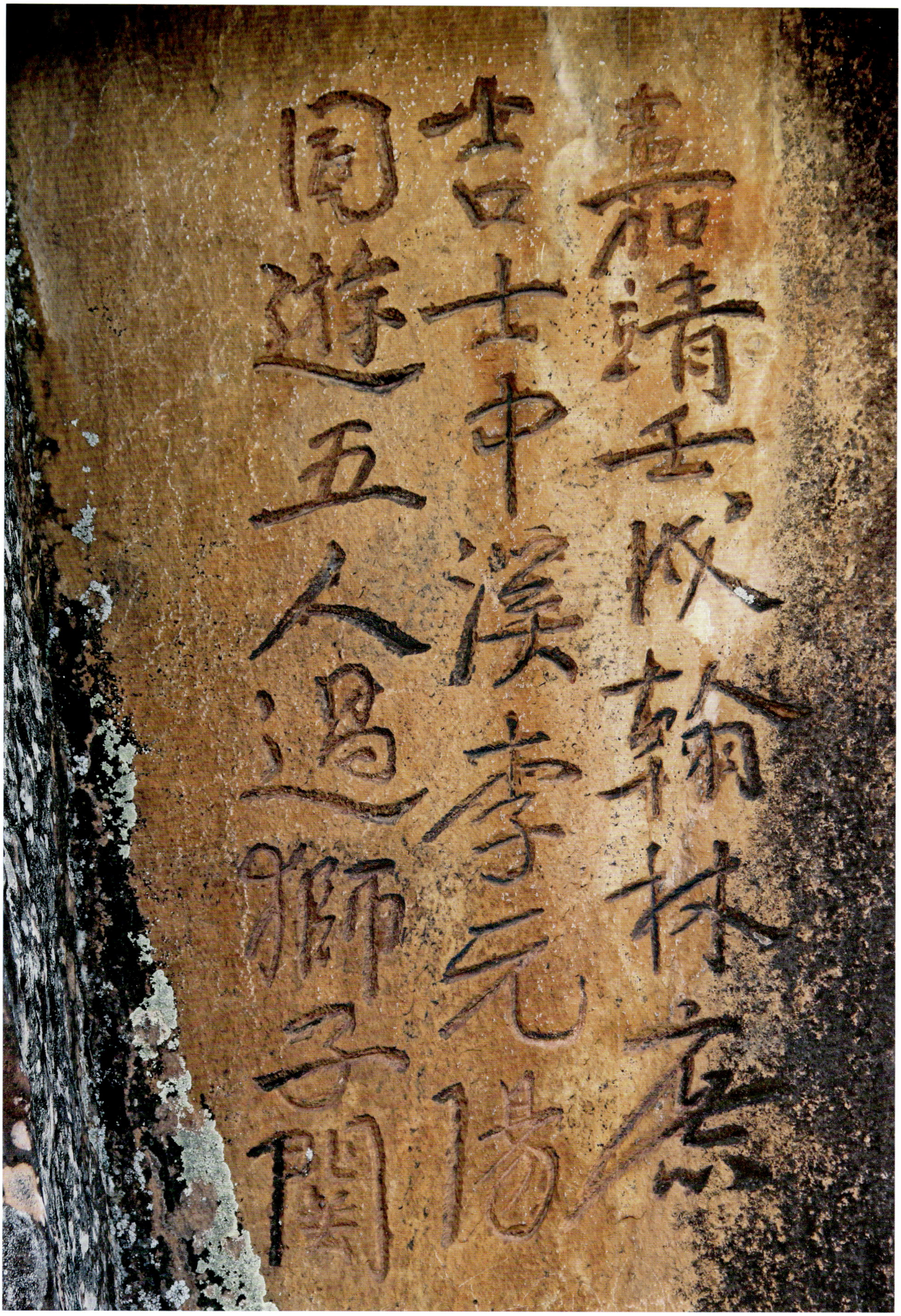

李元阳题刻 Li Yuanyang's Inscription

第三节　茶马古道遗迹

从史前时代开始，沙溪就是云南青铜文明的发祥地之一。在现代交通出现之前的两千多年间，沙溪一直是云南腹地沟通西藏、四川乃至南亚的马帮交通线上的重要关隘。南诏以后，这里成为除了云南与西藏“茶马互市”之外，另一个重要的国计民生商品——食盐的集散地和马帮站口。据历史记载，沙溪西部的云龙诺邓盐井在汉代开始开采。唐代，剑川开采弥沙盐井，称为“傍弥潜井”。弥沙井位于沙溪以西的弥沙乡，距离沙溪只有马帮一天时间的行程，交通便利。此后历朝历代不断扩大采盐规模，并加强管理。元至元二十九年（1292），设剑川盐课大司。明永乐年间，乔后盐井开始开采，仍属弥沙井。至清嘉庆时，弥沙井产盐量已达五万九千余斤。民国初年，年产食盐近百万斤。据民国2年（1913）《滇西驿运报告书》记载:“滇西有九千余匹马，剑川有约千匹。弥沙、乔后、喇鸡鸣井等盐道上终年有马帮运食盐。”当时，沙溪每天都有大量马帮过往住宿。清雍正、乾隆时期，史料记载剑川“州之沙溪、甸尾有夜市”，可以想见历史上沙溪曾有相当繁荣的市场经济，从而带动了文化和社会各方面的发展。

"滇茶进藏"——重走茶马古道
"Yunnan Tea Enters Xizang"—Re-walk the Historic Tea and Horse Caravan Trail

古道遗迹　Relics of the Ancient Road

沙溪由于处在联系滇西四大盐井的交会之地，千百年来，马帮沿着黑潓江河谷，往南经洱源、大理可通昆明，往西经云龙、保山可到达缅甸，往北经剑川、丽江可到迪庆藏区，或往西北经兰坪、维西，进入西藏。直到1952年滇西公路南段（大理—剑川）修通前，在这里通行的仍是大量南来北往的马帮。此后随着滇藏公路的修通，千年的茶马古道逐渐衰落。

由于滇藏茶马古道长时间从沙溪经过，在此遗留了众多的历史文化遗迹。其中，沙溪境内的石钟山石窟是1961年国务院公布的全国第一批重点文物保护单位；沙溪寺登街作为茶马古道上唯一幸存的古集市，于2002年列入世界濒危建筑遗产名录；寺登街上的兴教寺是云南现存最大的阿吒力佛教密宗寺院，具有较高的历史文化价值和建筑艺术价值，于2006年被国务院公布为第六批全国重点文物保护单位；沙登箐的明代杨惠墓是省级文物保护单位；此外有段家登古戏台、长乐魁星阁、城隍庙大照壁、明代建筑段良府等6个县级文物保护单位……

古道赶马人　Sumpter on the Ancient Road

Section 3　The Historic Tea and Horse Caravan Trail

Shaxi has been one of the origins places for Yunnan bronze civilization since prehistoric ages. During the more than 2000 years before existence of modern transportation, Shaxi was always the important pass for horse caravan traffic line from middle of Yunnan to Xizang, Sichuan and even South Asia. After Nanzhao period, besides being "Tea-horse Trading" place for Yunnan and Xizang, it also became another important gate for horse caravan and distributing center for salt, the commodity which is related to national economy and people's life. According to the historic record, Nuodeng salt well of Yunlong was begun to dig from Han Dynasty. In Tang Dynasty, Jianchuan began to dig Misha salt well, and called it "Deep well beside Mi". Misha well is located Misha Country west of Shaxi, only one day trip from Shaxi for horse caravan, so the transportation is quite convenient. Afterward, the successive dynasties expanded the exploitation of salt and strengthened management. By the 29th year of Yuan (1292), a supervisor for salt was nominated in Jianchuan. During Yongle period of Ming Dynasty, Qiaohou salt well began to be dug, which was still belong to Misha well. By Jiaqing period

古道新生活　The New Life on the Ancient Road

of Qing Dynasty, the salt production reached more than 29500kg from Misha well. By early Republic of China, the salt production was near half million kilograms. According to the record on "Transport Report of West Yunnan" in the 2nd year of Republic of China (1913): "There are more than 9000 horses in west of Yunnan, and there are about 1000 horses in Jianchuan. There are caravans shipping horse caravan salt all year long on the of Misha, Qiaohou, Lajiming Well, etc." At that time, there were a lot of caravans passing and staying every day at Shaxi. In Yongzheng and Qianlong period of Qing Dynasty, it was recorded that Jianchuan "State of Shaxi, has night market at Dianwei", so we can imagine there were quite prosperous market economy in Shaxi history, which drove the development of all aspects of culture and society.

As Shaxi is located at the cross of four salt wells of western Yunnan, so for thousands of years, horse caravan go along Heihui River, go south, through Eryuan and Dali to reach Kunming, go west, through Yunlong and Baoshan to reach Myanmar, go north, through Jianchuan and Lijiang to reach Diqing at Xizang area, or go northwest, through Lanping

古道穿行　Pass through the Ancient Road

and Weixi, to enter Xizang. Until 1952, before the open of south section of west Yunnan highway (Dali-Jianchuan), there were still lots of horse caravan passing here from each direction. After the open of Yunnan-Xizang highway, the thousand-year-old Historic Tea and Horse Caravan Trail gradually vanished.

As the Yunnan-Xizang Historic Tea and Horse Caravan Trail went through Shaxi for a long time, numerous of historical and cultural relics were left here. Among these, Shizhong Mountain Grottoes in Shaxi territory was on the list of the first batch of Major National-level Protected Historical and Cultural Sites, which was published by State Council in 1961; the Shaxi Sideng Street as the only survival ancient fair on the Historic Tea and Horse Caravan

古道沧桑　The Vicissitudes on the Ancient Road

Trail, was put into the list of World in Danger Architectural Heritage in 2002; Xingjiao Temple on Sideng Street is the biggest existing Acharya Tantric Buddhist Temple in Yunnan, which has high historical and cultural value and architectural artistic value, was put on the list of the sixth batch of national essential cultural artifacts protection units, published by State Council in 2006; Yanghui Tomb, located at Shadengqing, is from Ming Dynasty and is province level cultural artifacts protection units; Besides, there are Duanjiadeng Ancient Opera Stage, Kui Xing Pavilion at Changle, big screen wall at Town God's Temple, Ming structures Duanliang Mansion and other 6 county level cultural artifacts protection units...

马帮沙溪行　Horse Caravan's Shaxi Travel

第四节　传统村落

至2020年，剑川有25个村落被列入中国传统村落名录，其中沙溪有7个，分别是寺登村、甸头村、段家登村、长乐村、鳌凤村、华龙村、石龙村。

寺登村因寺登街而得名，地处沙溪坝子中央、黑潓江畔。寺登街是沙溪古镇的核心区域，也是寺登村的中心地点。经明清两代的持续建设，寺登街形成以兴教寺、魁星阁带戏台为轴心，以古戏台正面四方街为中心的古集市。集市的南北巷道为古代茶马古道的主要通道和街巷。

甸头村坐落在沙溪坝最北边，石钟山脚下，东邻黑潓江，南通沙溪古镇，是从剑川县城到沙溪经过的第一个村子。村落不大，村中原有施家巷、中和巷、腾蛟巷、起凤巷四条巷子，“一正一耳”“三坊一照壁”“四合五天井”“一进几院”等建筑样式的白族传统民居有序地排列在巷子周边，这些民居大部分为两层土木结构楼房，白墙青瓦，木质门窗雕刻精细，照壁、墙壁及大

段家登村全景 Full View of Duanjiadeng Village

门两侧常施以彩绘，与沙溪田园风光相映成趣。村北建有一个集佛教、道教、“阿吒力”教于一体的代表性寺庙建筑群——慈荫庵和玉皇阁。

段家登村距今已有600多年的历史，它坐落于沙溪坝子东北端，华丛山山麓，西隔黑潓江与甸头村相望，毗邻沙溪寺登街旅游风景名胜区。眺望段家登村，房屋依山势、顺地形而建，错落有致地分布于黑潓江与华丛山中间，西北麓地势稍高，房舍斑驳的多为最早居住的段氏人家，南麓地势低处，多居住着后入住的杨姓人。如今村域扩大，两姓人家大多往东南方向扩展，形成目前的村落规模。最具有代表性的古民居为位于村子正西方的段家登古戏台，戏台始建于清乾隆年间（1736—1795），是沙溪镇为数不多的四层魁星阁带戏台式建筑。一层为铺面；二层是戏台；三层是小型休息厅；四层供奉“魁星”，“魁星”又称“文曲星”“九头魁星”。段家登古戏台为剑川县文物保护单位，现开发为“戏台会馆”。

长乐村位于沙溪镇西部，长乐魁星阁、三教寺等与传统民俗相关建筑保留较多，古村落风貌完整，有浓烈的民俗遗风。

鳌凤村位于沙溪古镇西南，村庄西高东低，前有黑潓江畔的千亩良田，后有青山梯田果林。自古以来，鳌凤村是盐马古道和茶马古道上的重要驿站，商贾马帮往来穿梭。村子往西是绵延的大山，大山深处有个集哨所和文书传递为一身的重要驿站——马坪关，一直是弥沙盐井通往东面的重要关隘，又是兰州（今马登镇）通往沙溪、洱源等地的必经要塞。

华龙村位于黑潓江东岸、华丛山脚下，是沙溪坝子东面的风景林带和水源涵养林带，景色优美，有不少具有旅游开发价值的景点,其中“龙门箐”“三大塘”“华丛山顶峰”等景点特色鲜明。白族、彝族世代和睦相处，两个民族都能歌善舞，在传统节日和各种文艺会演中民族歌舞表演深受人们的喜爱。华龙村最著名的庙宇是回龙庵。

石龙村位于国家AAAA级旅游景区剑川石宝山腹地，有霸王鞭、三弦、白族调、洞经音乐、乡戏等白族民间歌舞乐。每年石宝山歌会期间，村里的群众都是歌会节白族调对唱比赛的主力军，歌手屡屡夺魁，堪称一绝。该村有剑川白曲、石宝山歌会、霸王鞭等代表性“非遗”项目，有李宝妹、李根繁、姜伍发、李繁昌等30多名代表性传承人。石龙的民居建筑形式上虽仍以传统的“三坊一照壁”为主，但区别于剑川其他地区的是，村里还保留有用云南松原木垒造的“垛木房”。此外，村内还有本主庙、观音庙、关圣宫、古戏台、土地山神庙等8处保存尚好的庙宇古建筑。

鳌凤村　Aofeng Village

甸头村 Diantou Village

长乐村 Changle Village

华龙村　Hualong Village

华龙村概貌 General View of Hualong Village

Section 4 Traditional Villages

By 2020, in Jianchuan, there had been 25 villages being listed in China Traditional Village List, respectively were Sideng Village, Diantou Village, Duanjiadeng Village, Changle Village, Aofeng Village, Hualong Village and Shilong Village.

Sideng Village, named after Sideng Street, is located in the center of Shaxi Basin and beside Heihui River. Sideng Street is the center area of Shaxi Ancient Town, also is the center of Sideng Village. Being continuously built in Ming and Qing Dynasties, Sideng Street was formed into an ancient county fair, with Xingjiao Temple and Kui Xing Pavilion with opera stage as the axis, the Ancient Opera Stage in front of Sifang Street as the center. The north-south lane of bazaar is the main street and pass of the Historic Tea and Horse Caravan Trail.

Diantou Village, located at the furthest north of Shaxi Basin, at the foot of Shizhong Mountain, Heihui River to the east, Shaxi Ancient Town to the south, is the first village going from Jianchuan County to Shaxi. The village is small, there were Shijia Lane, Zhonghe Lane, Tengjiao Lane, Qifeng Lane four lanes, "One Main Building with One Annexe" "Three Suites with One Decorate Wall", "Four Yards with Five Patios" "One Entrance

传统村落——寺登村　Traditional Village—Sideng Village

修复后的寺登街　Renovated Sideng Street

Several Yards", etc., these Bai Nationality traditional residence building types orderly stand around the lanes, and they are mostly two-floor buildings made of earth and wood, with white walls and grey tiles, delicate carved wooden doors and windows, colorful painted screen walls, walls and two sides of gates, all these scenes perfectly match Shaxi pastoral scenery. At north of the village, Ciyin Nunnery and Jade Emperor Pavilion was built there, as a representative temple group, which being integrated with buddhism, taoism and "Acharya" religion.

Duanjiadeng Village, with a history of more than 600 years, is located at the northeast end of Shaxi Basin, foot of Huacong Mountain, to the west, facing Diantou Village opposite to Heihui River, next to the Shaxi Sideng Street Tourist Scenic Spot. Looking from a distance, the buildings of Duanjiadeng Village are built along the terrain and mountain, scattered between Heihui River and Huacong Mountain, a bit high at the northwest end, the mottled houses were family Duan's Dwellings, which lived here at the earliest time, a little low at the south end, mostly lived by family Yang, who moved here later. Nowadays, the village get enlarged, two families mostly expend to southeast, forming the current village. Duanjiadeng Ancient Opera Stage, located at the west of the village, the most representative ancient dwellings, started building in Qianlong period (1736-1795), is quite few four-floor Kui Xing Pavilion with opera stage type building in Shaxi Town.

The first floor is shop; the second floor is opera stage; the third floor is small sitting room; the fourth floor is to worship "Kui Xing", who is also called "Wenquxing" "Nine-head Kui Xing". Duanjiadeng Ancient Opera Stage is Jianchuan County cultural relic protection unit, now is developed as "Opera Stage Guild Hall".

Changle Village, located at west of Shaxi Town reserves more buildings related to traditional customs, like Changle Kui Xing Pavilion, Sanjiao Temples, etc., with complete ancient village features and heavy customs heritage.

Aofeng Village, located at southwest of Shaxi Ancient Town, is higher at west and lower at east, in front, there are thousands Mu of fertile land beside Heihui River, at back, there are green mountains, terraces and fruit forests. Since ancient times, Aofeng Village has been an important post on the Historic Salt and Horse Caravan Trail and the Historic Tea and Horse Caravan Trail, with caravans shuttling around. West of the village is stretching mountains, Mapingguan, an important pass which integrates watchhouse with document delivery stands in the deep heart of the mountain, is always an important pass from Shami salt well to the east, and is also a key fort from Lanzhou (Now is Madeng Village) to Shaxi, Eyuan and other places.

Hualong Village, located at east side of Heihui River, foot of Huacong Mountain, is the scenic forest belt and water conservation forest belt in the east of Shaxi Basin, the sights are very beautiful, with a lot of sceneries worthy for tourism development, among these, "Longmenqing" "Sandatang" "Peak of Huacong Mountain" are with distinctive features. The Bai Nationality and Yi Nationality have lived here in harmony for generations, and both of them are good at singing and dancing, nationality dancing and singing are deeply loved by people during traditional festivals and various artistic performances. The most famous temple at Hualong Village is Huilong Nunnery.

Shilong Village, located in the deep heart of Jianchuan Mount Shibao, AAAA-Level National Scenic Area, famous for Bai Nationality songs, dance and music like Bawang whip, Sanxian, Bai

Nationality tone, Dongjing music, County play, etc. Every year, during Mount Shibao singing party, the villagers play main roles in the Bai Nationality tone antiphonal singing competition on it, singers repeatedly win champion for their fabulous performance. There are representative intangible cultural heritage programs like Jianchuan Bai Nationality music, Mount Shibao singing party and Bawang whip, and there are also more than 30 representative inheritors like Li Baomei, Li Genfan, Jiang Wufa, Li Fanchang, etc. The architectural form of Shilong Dwelling is based on traditional "Three Suites with One Decorate Wall", but what different from Jianchuan other areas is that "Duomu Houses" made of Yunnan pine logs are still kept in the village. Besides, there are eight well preserved ancient temples like Local Deity Temple, Avalokitesvara Temple, Guansheng Palace, Ancient Opera Stage and the Land God, etc.

寺登街一角　A Corner of Sideng Street

石龙村　Shilong Village

寺登街欧阳大院大门　The Gate of Family Ouyang's Yard on Sideng Street

第五节　特色建筑

沙溪古镇至今仍保存有完整的古老建筑，如古民居、古戏台、寺庙、寨门等。白族民居风貌古朴，古建筑结构造型别具一格。人们走进沙溪，幽思怀古，可以触摸到历史的脉动。

Section 5　Unique Architectures

By now, Shaxi Ancient Town still keeps the well preserved old and ancient buildings, like ancient dwellings, Ancient Opera Stage, temples, village gate, etc. Bai Nationality dwellings are full of ancient and simple features, and ancient buildings are with unique structures. When people walk into Shaxi, quietly thinking and missing the old days, they can feel the pulse of history.

鳌凤村民居大门　The Gate of Aofeng Village Folk Houses

一、传统民居

沙溪传统的民居建筑为三坊一照壁、四合五天井、平房带闷楼、前铺后院，其融汇了白族、汉族、藏族等民族建筑的一些优点而形成，古朴素雅、造型优美、组合灵活，特别重视庭院绿化和厦子（檐廊）的多功能利用，注重入口和山墙的多功能处理，在平面形式、建筑艺术等方面都有鲜明的地方特色与民族风格。

沙溪民居既保留了白族民居的一般特点，如封火墙、照壁等建筑元素，同时具有鲜明的本土特点。沙溪民居与周围山水自然环境浑然天成，外观具有质朴浑厚的地域特色，内部梁架形态随木料形状常会有曲梁的应用。传统建筑以三开间两层楼为一坊，双坡屋顶，悬山和硬山皆有。传统建筑的承重体系以木结构为主，土坯墙则作为围护体系，屋顶为小青瓦。建筑的主要建造材料以当地的木、石、土为主，建筑外墙以土坯色与红褐色为主色调，屋顶以灰色为主。注重与周边自然环境融合，正房主朝向，以坐西向东居多，整体布局因地制宜，院落组合方式灵活多变。古民居以寺登街的欧阳大院和赵氏家宅为代表。

寺登街欧阳大院　Family Ouyang's Yard on Sideng Street

白族传统民居院落——赵氏家宅一角　Bai Nationality Traditional Dwellings—A Corner of Zhao's House

1. Traditional Dwellings

Shaxi traditional dwellings include three suites with one decorate wall, four yards with five patios, bungalow with blind-story, front-shop back-yard, which integrates Bai, Han, Zang national architecture's advantages to form, ancient and full of elegant simplicity, beautifully designed, neatly assembled, especially take yard greening and multi-functional utilization of Shazi (Eaves) into account, also the multi-functional treatment at gates and gable walls, there are distinct local features and national styles on layout form and architectural technique.

Shaxi dwellings not only keep general features of Bai Nationality dwelling, like firewall, screen wall and other architectural element, also have distinct local feature. Shaxi dwellings integrate with surrounding natural environment, whose appearance has heavy and artless territorial feature, inner beam frame's shape exists application of curved beam adopt to the shape of timber. Traditional architectures take three bays with two-floor building as a suite, double pitch roof, both overhanging gable and flush gable. The load-bearing system of traditional architectures is mainly timber structure, adobe wall as enclosure system, blue roofing tiles as roof. The building's main construction material is local wood, stone and earth, the out wall of the building use adobe color and red brown color as basis, the roof is mainly grey. Emphasizing the integration with surrounding natural environment, the orientation of owner's room mostly standing west facing east, the overall layout adjusts according to local condition, yard's combination is flexible and varied. Ancient dwelling's representative is family Ouyang's yard and family Zhao's house.

甸头村民居　The Dwellings at Diantou Village

沙溪白族庭院大门　The Yard Gate of Bai Nationality in Shaxi Town

石龙村木楞房　The Wood House at Shilong Village

修复后的寺登街古戏台　The Renovated Ancient Opera Stage on Sideng Street

修复后的寺登街古戏台 The Renovated Ancient Opera Stage on Sideng Street

二、古戏台、魁星阁

古镇沙溪可谓村村有魁星阁、寨寨有戏台，从进入沙溪坝子的第一个村甸头起，19座戏台、魁星阁似点点繁星装饰着沙溪坝子。这些戏台、魁星阁从远古走来，见证了茶马古道的荣辱兴衰，向来往的游人讲述着属于每一个村寨古老而真实的历史。沙溪19座古戏台、魁星阁中，至今保存完好的有11座，其中以寺登街古戏台（魁星阁带戏台）最具代表性。

石龙村古戏台　The Ancient Opera Stage at Shilong Village

城隍庙古戏台　The Ancient Opera Stage at Town God's Temple

鳌凤村魁星阁　Kui Xing Pavilion at Aofeng Village

北龙村魁星阁 Kui Xing Pavilion at Beilong Village

2. Ancient Opera Stage, Kui Xing Pavilion

There are Kui Xing Pavilion and opera stage at every village in Shaxi Ancient Town, from the first village—Diantou Village when we enter into Shaxi Basin, there are 19 opera stages and Kui Xing Pavilion decorating Shaxi Basin like stars. These Kui Xing Pavilion and opera stage, approaching from ancient days, have witnessed the rise and fall of the Historic Tea and Horse Caravan Trail, telling the visitors of ancient and real history of every village. Among the 19 Ancient Opera Stages and Kui Xing Pavilion in Shaxi, 11 of them are perfectly well-preserved by now, Sideng Street Ancient Opera Stage (the opera stage of Kui Xing Pavilion) is the best representative one.

段家登村魁星阁带戏台　Kui Xing Pavilion with Opera Stage at Duanjiadeng Village

长乐村魁星阁　Kui Xing Pavilion at Changle Village

灯塔村魁星阁　Kui Xing Pavilion at Dengta Village

灯塔村戏台　The Ancient Opera Stage at Dengta Village

寺登街兴教寺　Xingjiao Temple on Sideng Street

三、庙宇

“本主”崇拜是白族特有的宗教信仰和民俗，也是沙溪最广泛、传统的信仰。历史上，在沙溪就有“沙溪十八村，村村有本主”的说法。唐宋时期，沙溪作为南诏、大理国茶马古道上的一个古镇，儒教、道教、佛教等不同宗教沿着古道进入沙溪，并在这里落地生根，与白族本土本主信仰共生共存，形成古镇独有的“三里不同寺，处处有香火”的独特景观。

鳌凤村印月庵　Yinyue Nunnery at Aofeng Village

3. Temple

"Local Deity" worship, is Bai Nationality's unique religious beliefs and customs, as well as the most popular and traditional belief in Shaxi. In history, there was a saying in Shaxi that "There are 18 villages in Shaxi, and each has its own Local Deity". At Tang and Song Dynasty, Shaxi, as an ancient town on Nanzhao and Dali Historic Tea and Horse Caravan Trail, Confucianism, Taoism, Buddhism and other religions got entered here along the ancient road, landing and rooting here, coexisting with Bai Nationality Local Deity belief, forming unique scenery that "There are different temples, with incense everywhere" in ancient town.

寺登街本主庙　Local Deity Temple on Sideng Street

甸头村慈荫庵（一）　Ciyin Nunnery at Diantou Village (1)

甸头村慈荫庵（二）　Ciyin Nunnery at Diantou Village (2)

鳌凤村城隍庙　Town God's Temple at Aofeng Village

下科村玉皇阁 Jade Emperor Pavilion at Xiake Village

华龙村回龙庵 Huilong Nunnery at Hualong Village

四、古桥

在流经沙溪坝子不足20千米的黑漶江河道上，曾分布着大大小小近20座桥梁。桥梁不但数量多，而且建筑形式多样，有木架桥、铁索桥、廊桥、拱桥、藤桥、风雨桥等。

随着现代公路桥梁建设的日新月异，古道遗留的古桥随古道上的马帮渐渐退出历史舞台，只余寺登古镇前的玉津桥、江尾的石鳌桥、马坪关的风雨桥等几座古桥。

4. Ancient Bridge

There were nearly 20 bridges of all sizes distributed on the less than 20 kilometers Heihui riverway that flowed through the Shaxi Basin. There are not only numerous, but also diverse in architectural forms, such as wooden bridges, steel cable bridges, corridor-style bridges, arch bridges, rattan bridges, wind and rain shielding bridges, etc.

With the quick change of modern highway and bridge construction, the ancient bridges left on the ancient road faded out of historical stage together with the caravans on the ancient road, there left only several ancient bridges, like Yujin bridge in front of Sideng Ancient Town, Shiao bridge at Jiangwei and the wind and rain shielding bridge at Mapingguan.

修复后的马坪关风雨桥

The Wind and Rain Shielding Bridge after Renovating at Mapingguan

修复前的马坪关风雨桥

The Wind and Rain Shielding Bridge before Renovating at Mapingguan

马坪关魁星阁戏台
Opera Stage of Kui Xing Pavilion at Mapingguan

溪南村石鳌桥 Shiao Bridge at Xinan Village

寺登村铁索桥　Steel Cable Bridge at Sideng Village

玉津桥　Yujin Bridge

北寨门　The North Village Gate

南寨门　The South Village Gate

东寨门　The East Village Gate

五、古寨门

寨门，进出寨子的通道，通常较狭窄，为仅容两匹马同时通过的土坯墙门，表示进了此门就是集市。寺登古街有三门，东寨门（通往大理地区）、南寨门（连结古镇南面与西面的滇西盐井）、北寨门（通往西藏地区）。时过境迁，寺登街上的寨门在岁月中悄然逝去。2002年寺登街入选世界濒危建筑遗产名录时，三座寨门只留下饱经风霜的东寨门守护着古镇，后来沙溪复兴工程重建了南寨门和北寨门。

5. Ancient Village Gate

Village gates are the pass of getting in and out of the village, normally narrow, and are adobe wall gates only allowing 2 horses passing by at the same time, entering the gate means entering bazaar. There are 3 village gates on Sideng Ancient Street, the East Village Gate (Lead to Dali area), the South Village Gate (Connect west Yunnan salt wells at south and west of the ancient town), the North Village Gate (Lead to Xizang area). With time changing, the village gates on Sideng Ancient Street have been fading away silently. In 2020, when Sideng Street was recorded into the List of World in Danger Architectural Heritage, there left only the weather-beaten East Village Gate protecting the ancient town, the South Village Gate and the North Village Gate were rebuilt by Shaxi Rehabilitation Project team later.

白族传统民居院落——三坊一照壁　Bai Nationality Traditional Dwelling—Three Suites with One Decorate Wall

六、其他

白族民居建筑有独特的风格，住房多采用“三坊一照壁”“四合五天井”样式。白族人重视门楼建筑和照壁、门窗雕刻及山墙彩画的装饰艺术。门楼装饰，通常采用泥塑、木雕、彩画、石刻、大理石屏凸花砖和青砖等组成串角飞檐，花枋精巧，斗拱重叠，雄浑稳重，美观大方，体现了白族劳动人民的建筑才华和艺术创造力。

6. Others

Bai Nationality dwellings have unique features, normally use style like "Three Suites with One Decorate Wall", "Four Yards with Five Patios". Bai Nationality people attach great importance on decorative arts, like gatehouse buildings and screen walls, engravings on window and door as well as the paintings on gable wall. The decoration of gatehouse normally uses clay sculpture, wood carving, color painting, stone carving, marble screen with relief engraving tiles and blues tiles, to form the upturned eaves, delicate flower pavilion, overlapped pendentive, magnificent and stately, splendid and elegant, which all reflect Bai Nationality laboring people's architectural talent and artistic creativity.

白族传统民居天井　The Patio of Bai Nationality Traditional Dwelling

城隍庙大照壁　The Big Screen Wall at Town God's Temple

白族传统民居院落——走马转角楼　Bai Nationality Traditional Dwelling—Corridor Running through All Sides

欧阳大院内宅门头雕饰

The Engraving on the Door Lintel of Ouyang's Inner Chamber

欧阳大院木雕　The Wood Carving of Ouyang's Yard

沙溪白族民居照壁　The Screen Wall of Bai Nationality Traditional Dwelling at Shaxi

欧阳大院格子门　The Panelled Door of Ouyang's Yard

甸头慈荫庵古树（树龄 530 年） Ancient Tree in Ciyin Nunnery Diantou Village (Tree-age 530 Years)

第六节　古树名木

作为千年古镇，沙溪留有一大批古树名木，至今仍焕发出勃勃生机。这些古树名木不仅树龄长，而且种类多、树形美。如今，沙溪寺登街除了古老的街道、房屋、寺庙外，最吸引人的就是它们了。它们不仅见证着寺登街的古老历史，也为寺登街增添了风采，是珍贵的遗产。至2020年，这些古树名木都已被挂牌保护。

Section 6　Ancient and Famous Trees

As an ancient town with thousands of years' history, Shaxi still remains a large number of ancient and famous trees, which are still full of vitality till today. These trees are not only long in age, but also have multiple varieties and beautiful shapes. Nowadays, in addition to the ancient streets, old houses, archaic temples, the most attractive scenery in Shaxi is these attractive trees. They are precious heritage for human being which not only witness the ancient history of Sideng Street, but also increase its charm. All of these trees have been listed for protection by 2020.

沙溪白龙潭古树群（平均树龄 300 年）　Ancient Trees Group in Bailong Pond in Shaxi (Average Tree-age 300 Years)

兴教寺内的古玉兰树（树龄 300 年） Ancient Magnolia Tree in Xingjiao Temple (Tree-age 300 Years)

沙溪寺登街古柿子树　Ancient Persimmon Tree in Sideng Street Shaxi

沙溪鳌凤村古树群（平均树龄 320 年） Ancient Trees Group in Aofeng Village Shaxi (Average Tree-age 320 Years)

沙溪寺登街老槐树（树龄 316 年） Ancient Chinese Scholar Tree in Sideng Street Shaxi (Tree-age 316 Years)

寺登街南古宗巷古树（黄连木，树龄520年） Ancient Tree in South Guzong Lane Sideng Street (Chinese Pistache, Tree-age 520 Years)

第五章

复兴沙溪

Chapter 5
Rehabilitation of Shaxi

第一节　茶马古道上唯一幸存的古集市

沙溪古镇是滇藏茶马古道的必经之地和重要驿站，曾是运送和交易茶叶、药材、丝织品以及盐的重镇。

寺登四方街是沙溪的灵魂与核心，是沙溪商贸交易的中心。它位于沙溪坝子中央鳌峰山鳌头位置，依山傍水，是一个地理位置极佳的“风水宝地”，也是一个集寺庙、古戏台、商铺、马店、开阔的红砂石板街面、百年古树、古巷道、寨门于一身，功能齐备的千年古集市。寺登古街有三个门——东寨门、南寨门、北寨门，西边紧靠鳌峰山，无寨门。东寨门通往大理地区，南寨门连结古镇南面与西面的滇西盐井，北寨门通往西藏地区。经过寨门，一条狭窄、深长的古巷道悠然延伸，两边古朴的铺面静立在巷道两边。狭长巷道的尽头，是寺登的贸易中心——四方街。四方街似曲尺形，正街南北长约300米，东西宽约100米。其中，北部街东西长约100米，南北宽约50米，整个街面用红砂石板铺筑，街中心有两株数百年的古槐树（其中一株于2004年6月因根系枯朽而折倒）。

旧时，寺登街每隔三天有一个街市，各地的马帮在街市前一天就陆陆续续通过巷道来到这里，戏台上洞经古乐、白族霸王鞭舞、民歌表演已经开始。古戏台是寺登四方街上最有特色的建筑，位于四方街东面建筑群中央临街的位置，与西面兴教寺殿宇、寺门建筑成一中轴线，将古四方街平分为南北两半，从而为划定各类生意经营范围提供了实物标志。

寺登街在茶马古道上的特殊地理位置，使这里成为中原文化、南诏文化、吐蕃文化和东南亚、南亚文化的交会地，各种来源、类型、流向的文化因子与本土文化在此碰撞、交融、沉淀。

以兴教寺为中心的寺登街成为连接东南亚、南亚和中国云南、西藏古道上繁荣的集市。佛教、儒教、道教与白族原生文化的不断交流与渗透，使寺登街形成以兴教寺佛教密宗文化为核心，以魁星阁带戏台的儒家文化为重点，以白族的本主崇拜和民俗活动为衬托，融前铺后店的马帮文化为一体的古集市。

随着19世纪末现代公路网络的完善和交通工具的发展，曾经热闹非凡的马帮驿站沙溪因远离交通干线而逐渐衰落。当地具有约600年历史的古戏台、马店等得以保留，成为宝贵的文化遗产。

沙溪古镇的核心是寺登街，寺登街的核心是兴教寺。兴教寺建于明永乐十三年（1415），已有600多年的历史，是寺登街上现存最古老的建筑。

兴教寺由门楼、过厅、二殿和大殿依次构成空间逐渐扩大的三个院落，占地面积5000平方米，至2020年是中国保存规模最大、最有代表性的佛教密宗“阿吒力”寺院。兴教寺内保存的明代壁画深受中原绘画风格影响，又具有浓郁的地方民族特色，是中国西南边疆古代白族的绘画艺术瑰宝。兴教寺具有较高的建筑艺术与绘画艺术等历史文物价值，是寺登街上重要的历史文化遗产，2006年被国务院公布为第六批全国重点文物保护单位。

兴教寺原有的寺院大门和观音殿毁于民国10年（1921）洱源土匪到寺登街抢劫放火之时。当时二殿及厢房是寺登街古镇居民的积谷大仓，古镇百姓奋力扑救，二殿和大殿幸免于难。现在的兴教寺大门为2004年沙溪复兴工程恢复重建。

兴教寺对面的魁星阁带戏台建于清嘉庆年间，后来经过光绪六年(1880)、1947年、1987年、1990年、2004年(沙溪复兴工程)5次维修。其结构精巧而壮观，三层飞檐翘角歇山式建筑，飞檐翘角有14个，均施以彩绘。最高的第三层是魁

古巷深深 The Deep and Ancient Alley

星阁，上悬挂有“文光普照”的匾额，塑有传说中为国家寻求栋梁之材的魁星。中间一层两边增加了出角檐厦，作为戏台使用，底层作为商铺。别出心裁的建筑艺术和独特的风格设计使整个建筑集魁星阁、戏台、商铺为一体，扩大了戏台的功用。魁星阁带戏台是整个古镇的核心区，是人们唱戏、跳舞、耍狮的地方，更是白族优秀建筑的典范。

兴教寺题诗（一）　Inscription Poems of Xingjiao Temple (1)

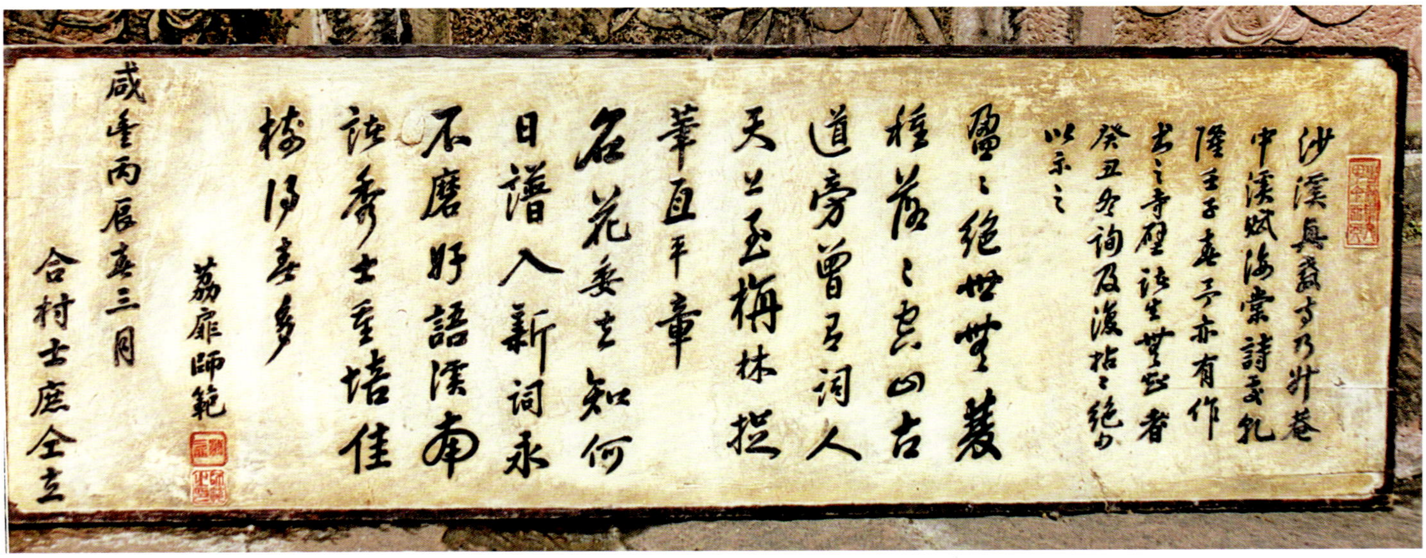

兴教寺题诗（二）　Inscription Poems of Xingjiao Temple (2)

兴教寺壁画《南无降魔释迦如来会图》　Mural of Xingjiao Temple "Shakyamuni Conquering the Demons" (Depicts a Feminine Shakyamuni Buddha Sitting on a Lotus Pedestal)

兴教寺壁画《太子游苑图》　Mural of Xingjiao Temple "Scenery of Prince Touring in the Garden"

Section 1 The Only Survival Old Market on the Historic Tea and Horse Caravan Trail

Shaxi Ancient Town is an essential place and an important postal stand for the Historic Tea and Horse Caravan Trail in Yunnan and Xizang. It was once an important town for transporting and trading tea, herbal medicine, silk fabrics and salt.

Sideng Sifang Street is the soul and core of Shaxi, and the center of Shaxi's business transactions. It is located at the head of Aofeng Mountain in the center of Shaxi Basin. With mountains and water surrounded, it is really a geomantic and treasure land due to its superior geographical position. Meanwhile, Shaxi Sideng was also an old market with complete functions which has thousands of years' history, for functional it has temples, Ancient Opera Stages, shops, caravansaries, for layout, it has wild stone slab streets made by red sandstone, ancient trees with more than hundreds years' tree-age, ancient allies and village gates. There are 3 village gates in Sideng Street: East village gate, South village gate and North village gate. No west village gate as it is closely near Aofeng mountain in west. East village gate leads to Dali area, South village gate connects salt wells in West Yunnan, and North village gate leads to Xizang area. Passing through the village gate, you will find a long but deep alleyway stretches leisurely, and the quaint pavements on both sides quietly stand on both sides. At the end of the long and narrow alley, it is Sifang Street which is the

寺登村旧貌 The Old Appearance of Sideng Village

寺登街铺面 Shops in Sideng Street

trading center of Sideng. Sifang Street is like a curved square with 300 meters long from north to south and about 100 meters wide from east to west. Among them, the north street is paved with red stone slabs entirely which is 100 meters long from east to west and 50 meters wide from north to south. In the center of it there are two big Chinese scholar trees which tree-age is hundreds of years (One of which was broken and fell in June 2004 due to the decay of its roots).

In the ancient times, there was a market every three days in Sideng Street. Caravans from various places came here one after another through the alleys one day before the market day. On the Ancient Opera Stage, people were performing Dongjing ancient music, bless dancing with Bawang whips (A wooden chip with 4-5 holes which can make different sounds) and folk songs performances. The Ancient Opera Stage is the most distinctive building on Sifang Street in Sideng. It is located in the center of the building complex in the east of Sifang Street and very close to the street. It forms a central axis with the palaces and temple gates of Xingjiao Temple in the west, and bisects the ancient Sifang Street into north and south halves, thus providing physical signs for the delineation of various business scopes.

Due to its special geographical location on the Historic Tea and Horse Caravan Trail, Sideng Street has become an intersection of Chinese central plain culture, Nanzhao culture, Tubo culture, Southeast Asia and South Asia culture. Cultural factors of various sources, types and trends, blending and colliding with local culture and settling down. Taking Xingjiao Temple as its center, Sideng Street, has become a prosperous market on the Historic Tea and Horse Caravan Trail connecting Southeast Asia, South Asia, Yunnan, Xizang and India. With the continuous exchange and infiltration of Buddhism, Confucianism, Taoism and the original Culture of the Bai Nationality, Sideng Street has formed an

修复前的四方街　Sifang Street before Restoration

修复前的寺登街集市　Sideng Street Market before Restoration

ancient market with Xingjiao Temple Buddhist esoteric culture as the core, Kui Xing Pavilion with Ancient Opera Stage confucian culture as the focus, the Bai Nationality's local deity worship and folk activities as the background, and integrating with the front room as shop and back yard as warehouse's culture of the caravans.

With the supplement of modern highway network and the development of transportation tools at the end of the 19th Century, Shaxi, the once bustling caravan post stand, gradually declined because it was too far away from the main traffic lines. But it has allowed the preservation of the 600-years-history's local Ancient Opera Stage and caravan inns, and become a valuable cultural heritage.

The core of Shaxi Ancient Town is Sideng Street, and the core of Sideng Street is Xingjiao Temple. Xingjiao Temple, built in the 13th year of Yongle in Ming Dynasty (1415) and has a history of more than 600 years. Xingjiao Temple is the oldest existing building on Sideng Street.

Xingjiao Temple consists of gatehouse, hallway, second hall and main hall, forming three courtyards with gradually expanding space, covering an area of 5000 square meters. It is the largest and most representative Buddhist Tantric "Acharya" Temple preserved in China until 2020. The murals of the Ming Dynasty preserved in Xingjiao Temple are deeply influenced by the painting style of the Central Plain Culture and have strong local ethnic characteristics. They are the painting art treasures of the ancient Bai people in the southwest frontier of China. Xingjiao Temple has high architectural art value and painting art value and other historical relics value. It is an important historical and cultural heritage on Sideng Street, and was announced as the Sixth Batch of Major National-level Protected Historical and Cultural Sites by the State Council in 2006.

寺登街入口 Entrance of Sideng Street

看戏　Watching Plays

The original temple gate and Avalokitesvara Hall of Xingjiao Temple were destroyed in the 10th year of the Republic of China (1921) when some bandits from Eryuan went to Sideng Street to loot and set fire. At that time, the second hall and the wing rooms were taken as granary of the residents who lived in Sideng Street Ancient Town. To save their grains, these residents fought hard with the bandits, and therefore the second hall and the main hall survived from this robbery. The current Xingjiao Temple gate was restored and rebuilt in 2004 in Shaxi Rehabilitation Project.

The Kui Xing Pavilion together with Ancient Opera Stage is opposite Xingjiao Temple, it was built during Jiaqing period of the Qing Dynasty, and later had been repaired for five times: in the sixth year of Guangxu period (1880), in 1947, in 1987, in 1990 and in 2004 (Shaxi Rehabilitation Project). It is a pavilion style building with three floors and its structure is exquisite and spectacular. All the three floors are decorated with eave hipped-roofs, and it totally has 14 cornices which are all covered with colorful paintings. The 3rd floor is also the highest floor, it is a special place for people to worship Kui Xing, (Kui Xing is a god in Chinese legend who can discover talents for the country), there is a plaque with the inscription of "Wisdom Star Light Shines" hanging over the top, and there is also a statue of Kui Xing inside of it. Whenever there was an imperial examination, students would come to worship Kui Xing to bless them to get good grades and become useful talents for the country. Corner eaves are added to both sides of the middle floor, which is used as an Ancient Opera Stage, and the ground floor is used as a shop. Ingenious architectural art and unique style design make the whole building integrate Kui Xing Pavilion, Ancient Opera Stage and shop, expanding its function of as only an Ancient Opera Stage. Kui Xing Pavilion together with Ancient Opera Stage is the core area of the entire ancient town. It is a place where people sing, dance and perform lion dancing. It is also an exemplar excellent architecture of Bai people.

南古宗巷 South Guzong Lane

古道赶马人 Sumpter on the Ancient Road

戏台新貌 New Look of the Ancient Opera Stage

第二节 中外合作保护古镇的典范

2001年10月11日，沙溪寺登街被列入世界纪念性建筑基金会(WMF)“2002年值得关注的101个世界濒危建筑遗产名录”。“中国沙溪寺登街（区域）是茶马古道上唯一幸存的古集市，有完整无缺的戏台、客栈、寺庙和寨门，使这个连接西藏和南亚的集市相当完备。”这句简单的描述从此改变了沙溪寺登街的发展轨迹，成了后来沙溪复兴工程的起点。

2001年12月，剑川县人民政府与瑞士苏黎世联邦理工学院签订《沙溪寺登街区域复兴规划备忘录》，共同组织实施“沙溪复兴工程”，项目主要包括沙溪古集市修复、周边村落的保护与开发、沙溪坝可持续发展、生态卫生与废物处理、扶贫与地方文化保护、宣传与交流等六部分。旨在通过构建一个涵盖经济、社会和环境在内的理想框架，在沙溪精心打造一个乡村可持续发展的范例。

2002年开始，经过剑川县人民政府的不懈努力，在瑞士苏黎世联邦理工学院等单位的全力支持下，中瑞双方搭建起合作平台，致力于文化保护与可持续发展的“沙溪复兴工程”全面启动。在双方的携手努力下，按照“修旧如旧、最少干预、最大保留”的理念复兴沙溪，通过沙溪复兴工程四期项目的开展，构建一个涵盖经济社会和环境在内的理想框架，给这个地方注入活力，使它恢复生机。这些各具特色的子项目都以当地人民及其相关的文化遗产、自然环境为重心，确立一种兼顾历史与发展的手段。整个工程关心的不仅仅是沙溪坝子的文化遗产保护，还有当地民众的现实需求。

2001 年剑川沙溪入选 WMF2002 年保护名录新闻发布会
Press Conference on Shaxi Market Area, Shaxi Valley, Jianchuan Yunnan China Selected for 2002 WMF List

对沙溪寺登街入选世界濒危建筑遗产保护名录作出贡献的人物进行表彰（剑川县表彰王亚军）

Recognition of People Who Contributed to the Selection of Shaxi Sideng Street to WMF List (Jianchuan County Honors Wang Yajun)

剑川县授予瑞士苏黎世联邦理工学院研究生米世文荣誉县民称号

Jianchuan County Honors Mi Shiwen, a Graduate Student at ETH Zurich, Switzerland, as an Honorary County Resident

沙溪寺登街第一期复兴工程中瑞双方修复专家及管理人员合影

Group Photo of Restoration Experts and Management Officials from China and Switzerland for the First Phase of the Shaxi Sideng Street Restoration Project

试点大门修复前后　Before and after the Restoration of the Pilot Gate

试点房修复前后　Before and after the Restoration of the Pilot House

修复前的兴教寺大门　The Gate of Xingjiao Temple before Restoration

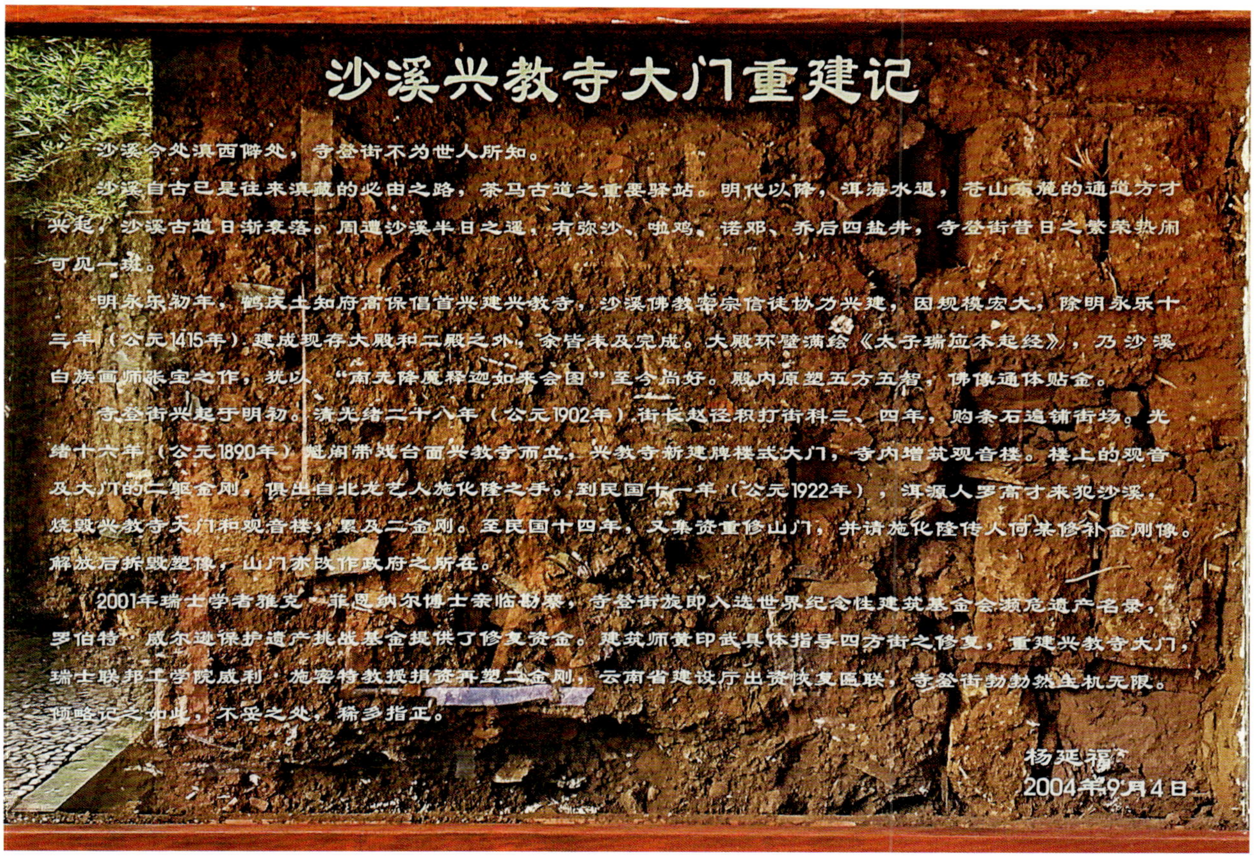

兴教寺大门重建记碑 Xingjiao Temple Gate Reconstruction Memorial Stone

修复后的兴教寺大门 The Gate of Xingjiao Temple after Restoration

修复前的南寨门　The South Village Gate before Restoration

修复后的南寨门　The South Village Gate after Restoration

修复前的兴教寺大殿　The Main Hall of Xingjiao Temple before Restoration

修复后的兴教寺大殿　The Main Hall of Xingjiao Temple after Restoration

修复前的兴教寺二殿　The Second Hall of Xingjiao Temple before Restoration

修复后的兴教寺二殿　The Second Hall of Xingjiao Temple after Restoration

修复前的古戏台 The Ancient Opera Stage before Restoration

修复中的古戏台 The Ancient Opera Stage under Restoration

修复后的古戏台 The Ancient Opera Stage after Restoration

修复前的四方街　Sifang Street before Restoration

修复后的四方街　Sifang Street after Restoration

Section 2 A Model of Sino-Foreign Cooperation in Protecting Ancient Towns

On October 11, 2001, Shaxi Sideng Street was listed in the "World Monuments Watch List of 101 Most Endangered Sites in 2002" by the World Monument Fond (WMF). Shaxi Sideng Street (Area) of China is the only surviving ancient market on the Historic Tea and Horse Caravan Trail. It has complete facilities including Ancient Opera Stages, inns, temples and fortress gates, making this market can adequately and completely connect Xizang and South Asia". The simple description in this sentence has changed the development track of Shaxi Sideng Street since then, and became the beginning of the later Shaxi Rehabilitation Project.

In December 2001, the People's Government of Jianchuan County and the Swiss Federal Institute of Technology in Zurich signed the "Shaxi Sideng Street Revitalization Planning Memorandum" to jointly organize the implementation of the "Shaxi Rehabilitation Project". The project mainly includes six parts: the restoration of Shaxi ancient market, protection and development of the villages in surrounding area, sustainable development of Shaxi Basin, ecological sanitation and waste disposal, poverty alleviation and local cultural protection, publicity and exchange. The aim of this project is to build an example of rural sustainable development in Shaxi by constructing an ideal framework covering the economy, society and environment.

外国专家考察四方街 Foreign Experts Inspecting Sifang Street

Since 2002, with the unremitting efforts of the The People's Government of Jianchuan County and the full support of the Swiss Federal Institute of Technology in Zurich and other organizations, China and Switzerland have built a platform for cooperation and fully started the "Shaxi Rehabilitation Project", dedicated to cultural protection and sustainable development of Shaxi. With the joint efforts of both parties, Shaxi will be rejuvenated in accordance with the concept of "Repairing the old as the old, minimum intervention, and maximum retention", and through the implementation of the total four phases of the Shaxi Rehabilitation Project, an ideal framework covering the economy, society and environment will be built, bring new vigor and vitality into this ancient town. These distinctive sub-projects all focus on the local people and their associated cultural heritage and natural environment, establishing a means of balancing history and development. The whole project is concerned not only with the protection of the cultural heritage of Shaxi Basin, but also with the practical needs of the local people.

In February 2003, the Sideng Street Water Supply Project, a sub-project of the Shaxi Rehabilitation Project, was launched. On February 18, 2003, Duanjiadeng Ancient Opera Stage began to be repaired firstly as part of the Shaxi Rehabilitation Project. In May 2003, the First Phase of the Shaxi Rehabilitation Project was launched. The Swiss side obtained funds through international channels, and the funds were about 7.53 million yuan, which was mainly used for the Swiss side's work expenditures and the restoration fee of ancient buildings. Swiss side repaired and restored a lot of ancient buildings, includes Duanjiadeng Ancient Opera Stage, East village gate of Sideng Street, Demonstration house, Gates for four old residential buildings, Sideng Street stage and its two-wing houses, ancient building complex of Xingjiao Temple, South village gate of Sideng Street, the street-facing shops around Sideng Central Primary School and other buildings' reparation. With the help and support from the state and the province, Jianchuan County has invested more than 8 million yuan in total, mainly used for infrastructure construction funds, publicity funds, housing property purchasing funds, and infrastructure construction funds in Sideng District. Jianchuan side Mainly completed construction of water supply project in Sideng block, construction of ecological parking lot, Water supply and drainage system in Sideng block, put strong and weak electricity wires and facilities into the ground, Pavement of road and street, pavement of north and south Guzong lane, tourist toilets and other projects. Both China and Switzerland side have carried out pilot promotion on the construction of ecological sanitation toilets, laying a solid foundation for the full implementation of the project.

On May 24, 2005, the People's Government of Jianchuan County and the Institute of National Regional and Local Planning of the Swiss Federal Institute of Technology Zurich signed a Memorandum of Understanding for Cooperation in Phase II of the Shaxi Rehabilitation Project in Kunming. The second phase of the project take the implementation of the "Mount Shibao-Sideng Street" Tourist Area protection and infrastructure construction national debt project as a key sub-project, this national debt project will be used for building tourist service centers, related streets restoration, building tourist toilets, make scenic greenings, make tourist signs and install garbage disposal facilities, etc. In addition to the national debt project, the second phase of the project also implements the restoration of the ancient market in Shaxi Sideng Street, management of the riverbank of the Heihui River segment that crosses the town, protection and development of surrounding villages; and focus on the maintenance of the ancient building complex of Xingjiao Temple and old caravan-inns, which are provincial-level protection sites; build a garden hotel in Sideng Street through investment promotion; formulate a sustainable development project plan for Shaxi Basin; implement a sustainable practice project for poverty alleviation at a world heritage site, improve the backwardness of tourism infrastructure in Shaxi Sideng Street as soon as possible; carry out tourism publicity and promotion to attract more tourists.

On the basis of the completion of the first and second phases of the Shaxi Rehabilitation Project, Jianchuan County and the Institute of Space and Landscape Planning of the Swiss Federal Institute of Technology Zurich signed a "Memorandum of Understanding for the Third Phase of the Shaxi Rehabilitation Project" in November 2007. The content includes investing more than 700,000 yuan to repair the main building structure of the Xingjiao Temple hall, investing more than 800,000 yuan to complete the installation of lightning protection, fire prevention and security facilities in the ancient buildings of Xingjiao Temple, and investing more than 400,000 yuan to complete two murals in

外国专家考察寺登街修复情况　Foreign Experts Inspecting the Restoration of Sideng Street

Xingjiao Temple. This experimental restoration of the murals in the main hall of the temple has founded the practical technical support for the restoration of the murals in the main hall of Xingjiao Temple. In addition, it also invested more than 600,000 yuan to complete the restoration and reconstruction of the "Five Wisdom From Five Directions" Buddha statues in the main hall of Xingjiao Temple, and invested more than 200,000 yuan to complete the requisition of the south courtyard of Xingjiao Temple and the purchase of wood for the management committee house as well as the compilation of "Shaxi Basin Regional Economic Development Strategy". The implementation and achievements of each phases of Shaxi Rehabilitation Project have played a positive role in building a local cultural tourism brand and developing the national cultural tourism industry.

On May 28, 2010, the Shaxi Rehabilitation Project. Jianchuan. China Inauguration Celebration for the Phase III and Understanding Signature Ceremony for the Phase IV were held at the Ancient Opera Stages on Shaxi Sifang Street. Diego Sameron, CEO of Swiss LEP Landscape and Environmental Planning Consulting Company, and the People's Government of Jianchuan County signed the Memorandum of Understanding for the

2004 年沙溪复兴工程第一期庆典活动 Celebration of the First Phase of the Shaxi Rehabilitation Project in 2004

Phase IV of Shaxi Rehabilitation Project. Both parties will continue to cooperate in the Restoration of the Buddha statues in Xingjiao Temple, detailed planning and preparation for the Shaxi Historic Tea and Horse Caravan Trail Museum and the protection and restoration of Sideng Village, and the overall Bai cultural heritage protection in Shaxi.

The important part of the Shaxi Rehabilitation Project is to development. For this purpose, they formulated "Shaxi Basin Regional Economic Development Strategy" In terms of agriculture, the development focuses on growing special crops, and producing organic food with national and international ecological signs; In terms of tourism, detailed and specific tourism development strategies and investment plans were formulated, highlight cultural heritage and picturesque pastoral scenery as the main potential for the development of tourism, and develop secondary tourism attractions (such as experience trails, hiking trails), create weather-independent tourism content (such as education activities, conferences, sports and health care services), construct and improve suitable tourism facilities.

On January 28, 2015, the signing ceremony of the Memorandum of Understanding (MOU) for the fifth phase of the Shaxi Rehabilitation Project was held at the Jiali Hotel, where Wang Yuan, Deputy Secretary of the County Party Committee and County Mayor, signed the MOU for the fifth phase of the Shaxi Rehabilitation Project with Diego Samelon and Huang Yinwu, CEO of Swiss LEP Landscape and Environmental Planning Consulting and head of the Swiss side of the Shaxi Rehabilitation Project. The focus of the project shifted from the restoration of ancient buildings to the preservation of traditional villages, improvement of the human environment, implementation of specific measures and the formation of a rural industrial system.

In 2003, the Shaxi Sideng Street area was designated by UNESCO as a Pilot Case Study within the framework of the UNESCO Project "Sustainable Management of World Heriatge Sites for Poverty Reduction", and in 2003, it received the World Monumental Architecture Foundation Award for Outstanding Achievement, and In 2005, the Shaxi Rehabilitation Project was awarded by UNESCO for "Award of Distinction, Asia-Pacific Heritage Awards for Cultural Heritage Conservation". In 2006, it was awarded the "Global Vision Award 2006" by Travel + Leisure and in November 2016, it was selected as one of the "2016 China Habitat Environment Model Awards".

沙溪复兴工程第三期签署仪式　Signing Ceremony of the Third Phase of the Shaxi Rehabilitation Project

沙溪复兴工程第三期完工庆典暨第四期谅解备忘录签署仪式
Shaxi Rehabilitation Project, Jianchuan, China Inauguration Celebration in Phase III and Understanding Signature Ceremony in Phase IV

2005 年文物保护培训会 Training Session on Heritage Conservation in 2005

沙溪复兴工程第五期合作谅解备忘录签字仪式

Signing Ceremony of the Memorandum of Understanding for Cooperation in Phase V of the Shaxi Rehabilitation Project

修复中的四方街　Sifang Street under Restoration

修复中的传统民居　Traditional Houses under Restoration

瑞士专家检查寺登街第一期工程修复项目

Swiss Experts Inspecting the Restoration Project of the First Phase of the Sideng Street Project

瑞士专家和县领导共商四方街兴教寺修复大计

Swiss Experts and County Government Leaders Discuss the Restoration Plan of Xingjiao Temple on Sifang Street

瑞士专家检查资助项目进展情况　Swiss Experts Check the Progress of the Funded Project

寺登街上的外国游客　Foreign Tourists on Sideng Street

第三节　遗产保护和开发

中瑞合作沙溪复兴工程开启了沙溪古镇遗产保护的新纪元。寺登街的保护范围为兴教寺、古戏台、旧商铺、马店、古巷道、寨门以及部分典型白族民居建筑。2000年，瑞士苏黎世联邦理工学院博士雅克·菲恩纳尔一行到沙溪寺登街，目睹的是一片衰败、凄凉的景象：古戏台摇摇欲坠，老宅东倒西歪，屋顶杂草丛生——正如雅克所言，这里“处于最绝望的失修状态”。2002年以后，剑川县人民政府与瑞士苏黎世联邦理工学院国家区域与地方规划研究所合作，实施以保护寺登街区域为核心的沙溪复兴工程。中瑞双方遵循国际文物修复的准则，以“修旧如旧、最少干预、最大保留”的理念，完成一至三期的关键性修复工作，在技术保护和社会影响两个方面均展示了较高的成就。沙溪复兴工程修复了濒危的白族民居和公共建筑，保护了厚重的历史文化和自然的田园风光，使沙溪成为中外游客向往的“诗和远方”。

旅游开发成果让沙溪古镇成为实现少数民族地区脱贫的样本。以民宿客栈经营为主体的旅游开发，提高了游客对沙溪白族民居文化遗产价值的认识、体验和了解，极大推动了沙溪经济社会的发展。据不完全统计，截至2020年底，沙溪古镇从事住宿、餐饮、木雕手工艺等各类经营活动的商家达200余家，其中80%以上的经营场所以当地白族民居建筑为依托，旅游业从业人数达5000余人。白族“非遗”传承人欧阳海育一家在老宅中开办三家巷客栈，主打白族人家生活体验、白族纸花“非遗”工艺体验和石宝山徒步等特色产业，在首批乡村旅游“千千万万”品牌评选活动中获得国家旅游局授予的“金牌客栈”称号。复兴工程成功实施带动的旅游开发成果，对

戏台夜景　Night View of the Opera Stage

悠闲时光　Leisurely Time

提高少数民族村镇群众的生活水平、实现脱贫致富起到了关键作用。

低碳社区营造缓解沙溪古镇核心区压力。2011年，瑞士驻华大使馆与剑川县人民政府签署《气候变化与对话合作谅解备忘录》，启动沙溪低碳社区项目。作为沙溪复兴工程的延续，由沙溪源乡村合作中心负责实施，低碳社区项目利用沙溪古镇城隍庙及周围空地建设，旨在建立绿色建筑试点中心、白族民俗活动中心。同时，进行石宝山—沙溪古镇低碳旅游景区和沙溪寺登街低碳旅游示范项目建设，鼓励和扶持沙溪古镇村民从事低碳徒步游的向导工作，并开展沙溪低碳旅游村庄导览路线和特色村庄的宣传推广。低碳社区营造对于缓解寺登村的旅游承载量，保护寺登街传统风貌，引领沙溪古镇乃至“全国生态县”剑川县的低碳绿色经济发展，进行了有益的探索，绿色可持续发展的效应正在显现。

Section 3 Heritage Conservation and Development

The China-Swiss Cooperation on Shaxi Rehabilitation Project has opened a new era of heritage conservation in Shaxi Ancient Town. The scope of protection of the Sideng Street is the Xingjiao Temple, the Ancient Opera Stage, the old stores, the caravansary, the old alleyways, the village gate and some typical Bai residential buildings. In 2000, when Dr. Jacques Fiennes and his team from the Swiss Federal Institute of Technology in Zurich visited the Sideng Street in Shaxi, they witnessed a decaying and desolate scene: the Ancient Opera Stage was crumbling, the ancient houses were falling down, the roofs were overgrown-as Jacques commented on here that "In the Most Desperate State of Disrepair". After 2002, the People's Government of Jianchuan County and the Institute of National Regional and Local Planning of the Swiss Federal Institute of Technology Zurich cooperated to implement the Shaxi Rehabilitation Project with the preservation of the Sideng Street area as its core. Both sides followed the international guidelines for restoration of cultural relics and completed one to three phases of critical restoration work with the concept of "Repairing The Old As The Old, Minimal Intervention And Maximum Preservation", demonstrating high achievements in both technical protection and social impact. The Shaxi Rehabilitation Project has restored the endangered Bai nationality residences and public buildings, preserved the rich historical culture and

2011 年沙溪低碳社区中心项目启动仪式举行 In 2011, the Launching Ceremony of Shaxi Low Carbon Community Center Project Was Held

natural idyllic scenery, and made Shaxi become a "Poetry and Distance" to which Chinese and foreign tourists desire to visit.

The results of tourism development have made Shaxi Ancient Town a sample of poverty alleviation in minority areas. The tourism development mainly based on the operation of the B&B inn has improved the awareness, experience and understanding of the value of the cultural heritage of the Bai people in Shaxi, which has greatly promoted the economic and social development of Shaxi. According to incomplete statistics, at the end of 2020, Shaxi Ancient Town engaged in accommodation, catering, wood carving crafts and other types of business activities amounted to more than 200 businesses, of which more than 80% of the business premises to the local Bai nationality residential buildings as the basis, the number of people engaged in tourism reached more than 5,000 people. Ouyang Haiyu, a Bai Nationality inheritor of intangible cultural heritage, runs the Sanjiaxiang Inn in the old house, which focuses on the life experience of Bai Nationality families, the Bai Nationality intangible cultural heritage of paper flower craft experience and the Mount Shibao trekking, etc. It was awarded the "Gold Medal Inn" by the National Tourism Administration in the first batch of rural tourism "Thousands Upon Thousands" brand selection activities. The tourism development results driven by the successful implementation of the Rehabilitation Project have played a key role in improving the living standards of the ethnic minority villages and towns, and realizing poverty alleviation and prosperity.

Low-Carbon community creation to relieve pressure on the core area of Shaxi Ancient Town. In

古镇夜色 Night View of the Ancient Town

2011, the Swiss Embassy in China and The People's Government of Jianchuan County signed the "Memorandum of Understanding for Cooperation and Dialogue on Climate Change" to launch the Shaxi Low-Carbon Community Project. As a continuation of the Shaxi Rehabilitation Project, implemented by the Shaxi Yuan Rural Cooperation Center, the Low-Carbon Community Project utilizes the construction of the Town God's Temple and surrounding vacant land in Shaxi Ancient Town, aiming to establish a Green Building Pilot Center and a Bai Nationality Folklore Activity Center. At the same time, the construction of Mount Shibao-Shaxi Ancient Town Low-Carbon Tourism Scenic Area And Shaxi Sideng Street Low-Carbon Tourism Demonstration Project is carried out to encourage and support residents of Shaxi Ancient Town to engage in guiding Low-Carbon trekking tours, and to carry out the publicizing and promoting of Shaxi low-carbon tourism village guide routes and featured villages. The Low-Carbon community creation has made a useful exploration to ease the tourism carrying capacity of the Sideng Village, protect the traditional style of Sideng Street, and lead the Low-Carbon green economic development of Shaxi Ancient Town and even the Jianchuan County—named as "National Ecological County", and the effect of green sustainable development is emerging.

非遗集市　Intangible Cultural Heritage Market

第六章

今日沙溪

Chapter 6
Today's Shaxi

第一节　基础设施建设

沙溪古镇有丰富的自然景观、丰厚的人文景观、得天独厚的区位优势，发展旅游业有巨大的潜力。但由于基础设施落后，宣传力度不足，沙溪旅游资源优势未能充分利用发挥。只有加大基础设施的投入力度，才有可能在加快沙溪城镇建设的同时，推动当地旅游业的发展。

为加大沙溪历史文化名镇的保护与开发力度，打造“茶马古道上唯一幸存的古集市”这一世界级建筑遗产品牌，各级政府为沙溪发展提供有力的政策支持，剑川县委、县人民政府和职能部门对剑川县沙溪中国历史文化名镇基础设施建设工程项目非常重视，在建设用地规划、行政规费减免、资金筹集等方面给予大量优惠政策，沙溪的基础设施建设迎来新局面。

2003年2月18日开始实施沙溪复兴工程，根据中国与瑞士双方签订的沙溪寺登街区域复兴规划备忘录，瑞方通过努力和积极协调，为沙溪寺登街复兴工程先后争取到境外资金人民币1600万元。同时，剑川县人民政府投资近2000万元，先后完成沙溪寺登街生态停车场建设，寺登街古戏台南北两翼房屋产权、老马店房屋产权购买并进行修复，寺登街场、南北古宗巷、东巷的铺装等基础设施建设。

2005年，沙溪复兴二期工程和石宝山寺登街基础设施建设项目启动。

2007年，沙牛公路弹石路改造完成，新建和改造乡村公路，建成沙溪客运站。

2008年，平甸公路剑川段油路改造项目总投资3600万元，12月30日全线通车。石宝山景区消防用水、三线入地和石钟寺至沙登箐游路等建设项目完成，与苏黎世联邦理工学院的合作进一步加强，沙溪复兴三期工程进展顺利，兴教寺大殿主体结构修复工程全面完工。

2009年，沙溪复兴三期主体工程全面完工。投资600万元，实施石宝山景区旅游基础设施建设项目。

2010年，加强小城镇建设。积极争取沙溪旅游小城镇建设资金，抓好寺登街水景建设和黑潓江过镇段沿岸的整治工作。完善乡镇商贸市场基础设施。加强城镇土地管理，清查乱建乱盖行为。完成农村集体土地使用权调查发证工作，妥善解决土地遗留问题。搞好土地收储，充分发挥土地在小城镇建设中的重要作用。狠抓城乡环境卫生综合整治。继续增加环卫、绿化投入，围绕广大群众普遍关心的市容市貌“脏、乱、差”问题，抓好城镇综合执法，增加环卫设施，清除卫生死角，改造破损路面，完善人行道路，拆除违章建筑，改善城镇的整体人居环境，提升城镇形象。切实抓好农村公益事业“一事一议”财政奖补工作，不断改善乡村人居环境。

2011年，沙溪中国历史文化名镇基础设施、沙溪中学改扩建等项目被列入国家投资计划。新农村建设扎实推进，沙溪中心集镇和2个中心村、3个示范村建设取得明显成效，完成投资2792万元。启动沙溪镇总体规划修编和寺登街控制性详规编制，对石钟山石窟保护房进行了修缮，石宝山—沙溪古镇创建国家AAAA级旅游景区顺利推进。沙溪复兴四期工程进展顺利，石龙村被评为第四批全省旅游特色村，旅游基础设施

水利资源 Water Resources

进一步完善。

2012年，沙溪镇抓住国家新一轮基础设施投资和“桥头堡”建设机遇，充分利用旅游小城镇发展、整村推进、重点村建设等契机，全镇续建项目6个，总投资1670万元，新建项目22个，总投资14804万元，争取申报项目15个，总投资55328万元。

2013年，黑潓江沙溪段治理项目可研通过省级评审。启动石宝山—沙溪古镇创建国家AAAAA级旅游景区工作，沙溪古镇游客服务中心建成投入使用。沙溪兰林阁酒店已完成主体建设，茶马古道文化体验服务中心开工建设。黑潓江沙溪段河道治理、金（华）沙（溪）高速公路PPP项目、扶贫开发整乡推进等重点项目前期工作扎实开展。

2014年，开展石宝山—沙溪古镇国家AAAAA级旅游景区创建。沙溪兰林阁等旅游服务项目主体工程基本完工。启动沙溪牲畜及特色农产品交易市场提升改造项目。启动县城到沙溪段高等级公路改造。

2014年9月，黑潓江片区剑川县沙溪镇扶贫综合开发项目启动。项目坚持连片开发与旅游发展相结合，结合沙溪镇情特点，按照“一乡一种风情、一村一个品牌、一寨一种模式”的要求，紧紧瞄准贫困村和贫困户，以14个行政村为主战场，以连片开发为平台，充分挖掘文化内涵，引导群众积极参与旅游扶贫开发，开拓产品，增强素质，培育自我管理能力，努力打造一批独具剑川特色的民族文化旅游村寨，推动贫困农户早日脱贫致富。项目批复总投资8272.45万元，主要用于基础设施建设、产业发展、美丽乡村建设、集镇功能提升建设、社会事业建设、生态环境建设。到位资金9955.35万元，累计完成投资9659.35万元，其中州、县财政专项扶贫资金7971.05万元，群众投工投劳折资及自筹1323.3万元。项目主要完成生态环境建设、基础设施建设，产业扶

乡村公路改造　Rural Road Renovation

贫、村内道路硬化及“五小”水利建设等其他项目有序推进。

2015年，黑惠江片区沙溪镇扶贫综合开发项目加快实施。剑川县正式启动沙溪国家级建制镇示范试点项目。项目围绕建设“白族生态文化旅游大景区”的目标，紧扣“世界濒危建筑遗产、茶马古道上唯一幸存的古集市、中国历史文化名镇”的定位，编制沙溪旅游发展规划和寺登街核心区详细规划，加快茶马古道文化体验服务中心建设。沙溪建制镇示范试点项目总投资3.62亿元。

2016年，沙溪国家级建制镇示范试点项目基本完成。加快实施以“一带一区十三村”为重点的美丽乡村建设，以城带乡、城乡融合发展格局初步形成。

沙溪建制镇示范试点项目总投资36231万元，其中中央专项补助资金6000万元，县级配套资金8248万元，整合部门资金21983万元。项目共5大体系，使用中央专项资金子项目21项，整合部门资金项目147项，建设年限为2014—2016年，分三年实施。项目通过探索城乡发展一体化体系，构建沙溪公共服务体系，建设综合信息平台体系，优化产业融合发展环境，完善乡村发展支撑体系。专项项目主要包括月牙潭湿地公园、“空心村”整治、城隍庙古旧建筑、茶马古道博物馆、低碳乡村游路、污水处理设施、垃圾热处理设施、马坪关关卡保护利用、客运站、特色农副产品交易市场等。建制镇整合项目完成93个，

黑惠江河道治理 Management of Heihui River

2015 年 10 月 28 日，剑川县在沙溪镇寺登街举行“刷卡无障碍示范街”启动仪式及宣传活动
On October 28, 2015, Jianchuan County Held the Launching Ceremony and Publicity Activities of "Cardless Demonstration Street" in Sideng Street, Shaxi Town

完成投资1.34亿元。

2016年12月，沙溪镇启动国家第三批新型城镇化综合试点工作。试点工作主要包含推进城乡一体化规划编制与管理、统筹城乡基础设施、打造智慧乡村、建设低碳社区、落实生态修复、发展低碳产业、探索多元化投融资机制、完善社会参与机制八个方面，涉及33个项目，总投资7.61亿元。

2017年，沙溪镇启动省级生态田园综合试点项目，围绕“农业增效、农民增收、农村增绿”和农村生产生活生态“三生同步”，一、二、三产业“三产融合”，农业文化旅游“三位一体”，积极探索推进农村经济社会全面发展的新模式、新业态、新路径。项目总投资2300万元。

2018年，沙溪古镇被列入2018年全省优秀特色小镇，获得1.5亿元奖补资金。沙溪镇鳌凤村省级农村综合改革乡村振兴试点示范项目启动实施，沙溪镇、沙溪镇鳌凤村被列入州级试点。

2019年，沙溪古镇成为云南首个5G商用试点特色小镇，数字化沙溪特色小镇运行良好，行政村光纤和4G网络实现全覆盖。“一部手机办事通”、ETC安装推广应用取得实效，智慧旅游、智慧政务、智慧城管、智慧水务建设逐步推开。

剑川县按照“国际化、高端化、特色化、智慧化”的原则，以“一部手机游云南”建设为契机，着力实施旅游厕所智慧建设，全面落实“旅游革命”任务部署。在旅游厕所的设计建造上采用白族传统的建筑方式，突出沙溪茶马古道马帮的文化特色。厕所内部配置智能取纸机、烘手机、感应式洗手液、感应式水龙头、挂钩等设施，并设有残疾人专用间、母婴专用间等人性化功能分区，让群众方便如厕。厕所智慧化后端通过与“一部手机游云南”平台连接，实现让游客拿着手机便可以查找、导航到最近的厕所，实时了解厕所的坑位占用、温湿度、空气质量、人流量等情况，从而优化厕所资源配置，提升游客体

田园综合体项目联合卧虹桥　Field Complex Project Joint Lying Rainbow Bridge

中心集镇主干道　Center Town Main Road

沪滇合作项目联合村跨黑惠江光明桥、光明路
Shanghai-Yunnan Cooperation Project Joint Village Across the Heihui River Guangming Bridge, Guangming Road

沙溪镇初级中学　Shaxi Town Junior High School

丰富的校园文化活动（一）　Various School Cultural Activities (1)

丰富的校园文化活动（二）　Various School Cultural Activities (2)

沙溪省级生态田园综合体项目　Shaxi Provincial Ecological Field Complex Project

低碳游道　Low Carbon Tour Road

Section 1 Infrastructure Construction

Shaxi Ancient Town has rich natural landscapes, abundant humanistic landscape, unique location advantages, there is a huge potential for the development of tourism. However, due to backward infrastructure and insufficient publicity, the advantages of Shaxi tourism resources have not been fully utilized. Only by increasing the investment in infrastructure, we can accelerate the construction of the town of Shaxi and promote the development of local tourism at the same time.

In order to increase the protection and development of Shaxi historical and cultural town, to create "The only Surviving Ancient Bazaar on the Historic Tea and Horse Caravan Trail", this world-class architectural heritage brand, governments at all levels to provide strong policy support for the development of Shaxi, the Jianchuan County Committee, the County People's Government and functional departments pay great attention to the Jianchuan County Shaxi Chinese Historical and Cultural Town infrastructure project, in the construction of land planning, administrative fee waivers, fund-raising and other aspects to give a lot of preferential policies, Shaxi infrastructure construction ushered in a new situation.

On February 18, 2003, the Shaxi Rehabilitation Project was started. According to the "Shaxi Sideng Street Regional Rehabilitation Planning Memorandum" signed bilaterally between China and Swiss, the Swiss side, through its efforts and active coordination, has secured foreign funds of 16 million RMB for the Shaxi Sideng Street Rehabilitation Project. At the same time, The People's Government

寺登街环境清理和检查 Cleanup and Inspection of Environment in Sideng Street

沙溪镇联合村文化活动广场附属景观　Landscape Attached to the Cultural Activity Square in Union Village, Shaxi Town

of Jianchuan County invested nearly 20 million RMB, and successively completed the construction of ecological parking lot on Shaxi Sideng Street. The ownership of the houses in the north and south wings of the Ancient Opera Stage on Sideng Street, the ownership of the houses in the ancient caravansary were purchased and repaired, and the infrastructure construction such as the paving of Sideng Street yard, north and south Guzong lane and east lanes were completed.

In 2005, the second phase of the Shaxi Rehabilitation Project and the Mount Shibao Sideng Street infrastructure construction project were launched.

In 2007, the renovation of Sha Niu Highway semi-neat stone pavement was completed, new and renovated country roads were built and Shaxi passenger station was completed.

In 2008, the Pingdian Highway Jianchuan section of asphalt road renovation project with a total investment of 36 million RMB, the whole line was opened to traffic on December 30. The projects such as Mount Shibao Scenic Spots fire protection water; electricity, communications, TV lines into the ground; Shizhong Temple to Shadengqing Road, and other construction projects completed. The collaboration with ETH Zurich was further strengthened, the third phase of Shaxi Rehabilitation Project progressed smoothly, and the main structure restoration project of Xingjiao Temple was fully completed.

In 2009, the main project of the third phase of Shaxi Rehabilitation was fully completed. Invested 6 million RMB to implement the tourism infrastructure construction project of Mount Shibao Scenic Area.

In 2010, strengthen the construction of small

towns. Actively strive for funds for the construction of Shaxi small tourist town, and ensure that the construction of the water feature of the Sideng Street and the rectification of the area along the Heihui River over the town. Improve the infrastructure of rural trade markets. Strengthen the management of land in towns, remove and deal with indiscriminate construction. Complete the survey and licensing of rural collective land use rights, and properly solve the legacy of problems. Make good land storage and give full play to the important role of land in the development of small towns. Pay close attention to the comprehensive improvement of urban and rural environmental health. Continue to increase the investment in sanitation and greening, focus on the general public's concern about the "Dirty, Disorderly and Unpleasant" city appearance, improve the comprehensive law enforcement of the town, increase sanitation facilities, remove the unsanitary nooks and crannies, renovate the damaged roads, improve the sidewalk, remove the illegal buildings, improve the overall living environment of the town and enhance the town image. Effectively seize the rural public welfare undertakings "An Issue with a Proposal" financial incentives, and constantly improve the rural living environment.

In 2011, Shaxi Chinese historical and cultural town infrastructure, Shaxi Middle School expansion projects were included in the national investment plan. New rural construction solidly promote, Shaxi central town and 2 central villages, 3 model villages construction achieved significant results, completed investment of 27.92 million RMB. Launched the Shaxi Town master plan revision and the preparation of the controlling detailed plan of the Sideng Street, the Shizhong Mountain Grottoes protection house

古镇环境提升整治 Ancient Town Environmental Improvement and Rectification

was repaired, Mount Shibao-Shaxi Ancient Town creating a National AAAA-Level Scenic Spot smoothly. Shaxi Rehabilitation of the fourth phase of the project progressed smoothly, Shilong Village was named the fourth batch of the provincial tourism characteristic village, tourism infrastructure to further improve.

In 2012, Shaxi Town to seize the new round of national infrastructure investment and "Bridgehead" construction opportunities, make full use of small tourism town development, the promotion of the whole village, the construction of key villages and other opportunities, the town continued to build 6 projects, with a total investment of 16.7 million RMB, 22 new projects, with a total investment of 148.04 million RMB, and strive to declare 15 projects, with a total investment of 553.28 million RMB.

In 2013, the study on the management of the Heihui River Shaxi section passed the provincial review. Start the work of Mount Shibao-Shaxi Ancient Town to create a National AAAAA-Level Tourist Attraction, Shaxi Ancient Town visitor service center was put into use. Shaxi Lanlinge has completed the main construction of the hotel, the Historic Tea and Horse Caravan Trail cultural experience service center began construction. River way management of Shaxi section of the Heihui River, Jinhua Shaxi Highway PPP Project, poverty alleviation and development of the whole township and other key projects to carry out solid preliminary work.

In 2014, the Shi Baoshan - Shaxi Ancient Town created a National AAAAA-Level Tourist Attraction. The main project of Shaxi Lanlinge and other tourism service projects was basically completed.

沙溪镇中心敬老院 Shaxi Town Center Elderly Home

智慧厕所　Smart Toilets

Launched Shaxi livestock and special agricultural products trading market upgrading project. Started the renovation of high-grade highway from the county to Shaxi section.

In September 2014, the comprehensive development project of poverty alleviation in Shaxi Town, Jianchuan County, Heihui River Area was launched. The project insists on the combination of continuous development and tourism development, combined with the characteristics of Shaxi Town, in accordance with the requirements of "A township a style, a village a brand, a village a model" closely targeting poor villages and poor households, with 14 administrative villages as the main battlefield, to link into a piece of development as a platform, fully explore the cultural connotation, guide the public to actively participate in tourism poverty alleviation development, to develop products, enhance the ability, cultivate self-management ability, and strive to create a number of unique Jianchuan features of the ethnic cultural tourism villages, to promote the early release of poor farmers from the poor to enrichment. The project approved a total investment of 82,724,500 RMB, mainly for infrastructure construction, industrial development, beautiful countryside construction, town function upgrading construction, social undertakings construction, ecological environment construction. The arrival fund is 99,553,500 RMB, and the accumulated investment is 96,593,500 RMB, of which 79,710,500 RMB are special poverty alleviation funds from the state and county, and 13,233,000 RMB are for the masses to participate in the construction discount wages and self-financing. The project mainly completes ecological environment construction, infrastructure construction, industrial poverty alleviation, village road hardening and "Five Small (small water cellars, small pools, small pumping station, small pond dams, small water channels)" water conservancy construction and other projects orderly advance.

In 2015, the implementation of the comprehensive development project to alleviate poverty in Shaxi Town in the Heihui River Area was accelerated. Jianchuan County officially launched the Shaxi national demonstration pilot project. The project revolves around the construction of "Bai Ecological and Cultural Tourism Scenic Spot" goal, closely following the "World's Endangered Architectural Heritage, the only Surviving Ancient Market on the Historic Tea and Horse Caravan Trail, China's Famous Historical and Cultural Town" positioning, the preparation of Shaxi tourism development planning and Sideng Street Core Area detailed planning, accelerate the construction of the Historic Tea and Horse Caravan Trail Cultural Experience Service Center. The total investment in the demonstration pilot project of Shaxi formed town is 362 million RMB.

In 2016, Shaxi formed town demonstration pilot project for the formation of the town was basically completed. Accelerate the implementation of the "One Belt, One Area, Thirteen Villages" as the focus of the construction of beautiful countryside, the city with the countryside, the initial formation of urban-rural integration development pattern.

The total investment of Shaxi formed town demonstration pilot project is 362.31 million RMB, including 60 million RMB of specific subsidies from the central government, 82.48 million RMB of county-level supporting funds, and 219.83 million RMB of integrated departmental funds. The project has 5 major systems, 21 sub-projects using the central government special funds and

寺登村墙体彩绘 Wall Painting in Sideng Village

147 projects using integrated departmental funds, and the construction period is 2014-2016, to be implemented in three years. The project explores the integration system of urban and rural development, builds the system of Shaxi public service, constructs the system of comprehensive information platform, optimizes the environment of industrial integration development, and improves the support system of rural development. The special projects mainly include Yueyatan Wetland Park, "Hollow Villages" Rectification, the old building of Town God's Temple, the Museum of the Historic Tea and Horse Caravan Trail, low-carbon countryside tour road, sewage treatment facilities, thermal waste treatment facilities, Mapingguan protection and utilization, passenger transport station, special agricultural and by-products trading market, etc. Completed 93 organic town integration projects, and completed investment of 134 million RMB.

In December 2016, Shaxi Town started the third batch of national comprehensive pilot work of new urbanization. The pilot work mainly contains eight aspects of promoting integrated urban-rural planning and management, coordinating urban-rural infrastructure, creating smart villages, building low-carbon communities, implementing ecological restoration, developing low-carbon industries, exploring diversified investment and financing mechanisms, and improving social participation mechanisms, involving 33 projects with a total investment of 761 million RMB.

In 2017, Shaxi Town launched the provincial ecological field comprehensive pilot project. The project focuses on "Agricultural Efficiency, Farmers' Income, Rural Greening" stay at pace with rural production, life and ecology, primary, secondary

新农村建设墙体彩绘 Wall Painting of New Rural Construction

and tertiary industries "Three Industry Integration" agricultural culture tourism "Trinity" to actively explore a new model, new industry, new path to promote the overall development of rural economy and society. The total investment of the project is 23 million RMB.

In 2018, Shaxi Ancient Town was included in the 2018 Provincial Excellent Specialty Small Town and received 150 million RMB award funds. Shaxi Town Aofeng Village provincial comprehensive rural reform Rural Revitalization Pilot Demonstration Project was launched, and Shaxi Town and Shaxi Town Aofeng Village were included in the state-level pilot.

In 2019, Shaxi Ancient Town became the first 5G commercial pilot feature town in Yunnan, the digital Shaxi feature town is running well, and the fiber optic and 4G networks in administrative Villages have achieved full coverage. "Cellphone does Things Through" ETC installation and promotion to achieve effective application, smart tourism, smart government, smart city management, smart water construction launched gradually.

Jianchuan County, in accordance with the principle of "Internationalization, High-end, Specialization, Smart", to "Travel around Yunnan with a mobile phone" construction as an opportunity to focus on the implementation of tourism toilet smart construction, the full implementation of the "Tourism Revolution" task deployment. In the design and construction of tourism toilets using the traditional Bai nationality architecture, highlighting the caravan cultural characteristics of the Shaxi Historic Tea and Horse Caravan Trail. The interior of the toilet is equipped with smart paper dispenser, hand dryer, inductive hand sanitizer, inductive faucet, hooks and other facilities, and there are humanized functional partitions such as special rooms for the disabled and special rooms for mothers and babies, making it convenient for the public to use the toilet. The back-end of the smart toilet is connected to the "Travel around Yunnan with a Mobile Phone" platform, so that visitors can find and navigate to the nearest toilet with their cellphones, and learn about the occupancy of the toilet, temperature and humidity, air quality, and the flow of people in real time, thus optimizing the allocation of toilet resources and improving the visitor experience. The electronic screen in the toilet takes into account the function of information release screen, and then accesses the scenic spot information management platform to support advertising, unified release and linkage of emergency contents, which is convenient for scenic spot operation and maintenance.

特色小吃市场建成 Special Snack Market Completed

From October 8, 2019 to January 23, 2020, Shaxi Ancient Town to implement infrastructure renovation and upgrading projects, implemented in 2003 to upgrade the Sideng Street pipe network project, during this period, the core section of the ancient town closed in batches of construction.

In 2020, in the development of "Remain true to our original aspiration and keep our mission firmly in mind" theme education, Shaxi Town from the perspective of promoting the long-term development of the town, the development of "Shaxi Town Tourism to Improve the Environment of Special Focused Action Implementation Plan" and other work programs, carefully sort out the difficulties and problems encountered in the development of Shaxi Ancient Town, one by one rectification, comprehensive improvement. Shaxi Town, removing a total of 360 pieces of uncoordinated and disorderly signs, 971 marketing advertisements, unified and standardized set hanging with Jianchuan characteristics, Chinese and English wooden store signs 258 pieces and 160 wooden couplets; a total of 5,000 square meters of new greening area, planting all kinds of flowers and plants 182,000; according to the standard of "See Light No Lights", 195 street lights were repaired and cleaned, 149 new street lights were built; all modern building facades in the main sections of the core area were transformed into Bai nationality residence facades, 37 uncoordinated building facade colors were rectified, and 5 unauthorized houses in the core area were demolished. The six main problems that constrain the development of Shaxi Ancient Town have been comprehensively rectified.

沙溪大牲畜交易市场 Shaxi Large Livestock Trading Market

沙溪客运站 Shaxi Passenger Transport Station

低碳交通线（一） Low-carbon Traffic Line (1)

低碳交通线（二） Low-carbon Traffic Line (2)

古道花海　Ancient Road Flower Sea

生态田园综合体项目局部　Part of the Ecological Field Complex Project

第二节 脱贫攻坚

2011—2015年，沙溪按照扶贫脱贫摘帽目标，以“五个一批”为抓手，打响新一轮扶贫攻坚战。完成扶贫专项工程投资885万元。实施长乐、华龙以及石龙后山彝族自然村整村推进项目，惠及贫困群众836户2910人。推进黑潓江片区沙溪镇扶贫综合开发工作，发放扶贫贴息贷款2300万元。扎实开展“挂包帮”[1]“转走访”[2]扶贫工作，州县镇对775户贫困户2632人进行两轮遍访，其间完成贫困户建档立卡“回头看”工作，退出建档立卡152户615人，进入187户615人。2015年，实现脱贫89户315人。沙溪积极实施易地扶贫搬迁项目，边远贫困山区扶贫攻坚战全面打响。

2016年以后，沙溪镇紧扣一次性高质量脱贫摘帽的目标任务，以攻坚措施和绣花功夫扎实推动各项扶贫政策措施落地生根。深入精准开展动态管理工作，2016—2020年，累计减贫824户3244人，实现6个贫困村出列，贫困发生率从2014年的12.44%降为0，实现高质量一次性脱贫摘帽。持续推进产业扶贫，烤烟、制种玉米、中药材、地参等优势产业稳步发展，旅游特色产业稳步推进，新型经营主体与贫困户利益联结机制进一步强化，带贫效果愈加明显；完成劳动力培训14期共3400人，劳动力转移3250人，其中转移建档立卡贫困人口1199人，办理建档立卡外出务工人员“一次性交通补贴”235人，贫困群众工资性收入占比明显提高；不断深化教育扶贫、健康扶贫，全镇3244人建档立卡，贫困人口100%参加医疗保险和大病保险，义务教育阶段学生无因贫辍学失学情况发生；全面落实住房安全保障，累计完成易地扶贫搬迁325户，实施完成四类[3]、非四类对象农危房改造536户，住房质量提升826户，贫困群众住房安全问题得到有效解决；完善农村安全饮水管理制度，全面推行入户调查、水质检测、设施配套、综合整治和提升认可度“五个全覆盖”，建立健全管水用水长效机制，全镇安全饮水得到全面保障；强化问题整改落实，累计整改清零上级各类巡视巡察和督查检查发现问题190个；做实做细村级施工图和镇级路线图编

剑川白曲宣讲团到沙溪开展脱贫攻坚政策宣讲

Jianchuan Baiqu Publicity Mission to Shaxi to Carry out Poverty Alleviation Policy Propaganda

① 挂包帮：是指省、市、县、乡四级干部整体联动，建立健全全省扶贫攻坚“领导挂点、部门包村、干部帮户”定点挂钩扶贫工作长效机制。

② 转走访：是在建立“挂包帮”长效机制基础上，全省统一组织开展“转作风走基层遍访贫困村贫困户”工作的简称。

③ 四类：1.农村低收入人口；2.省定经济薄弱村；3.扶贫开发重点片区；4.扶贫开发重点县（区）。

制，实行动态调整，挂图作战，努力补齐短板；强化宣传引导，深入开展“自强、诚信、感恩”宣传教育活动，持续推进“小喇叭、大广播，助力脱贫攻坚”工程，筹建14个“爱心超市”，激发群众内生动力，智志双扶。

2020年，沙溪镇通过第三方评估检查、脱贫攻坚普查验收和成效考核。后续始终坚持脱贫摘帽“四不摘”（摘帽不摘责任、摘帽不摘政策、摘帽不摘帮扶、摘帽不摘监管），注重返贫监测和持续帮扶，确保扶贫力度不减、投入不降、政策不变。一是提高政治站位，坚持脱贫攻坚统领工作全局，压实46名驻村工作队员、16支脱贫攻坚党员突击队和全镇干部职工决战决胜脱贫攻坚责任意识，确保主要精力始终聚焦脱贫攻坚工作。二是紧盯剩余贫困人口脱贫出列。聚焦“两不愁三保障”和安全饮水突出问题及贫困户脱贫5条标准，按“一户一方案、一人一措施”补齐全镇67户183人剩余贫困户、44户脱贫监测户、53户边缘户的短板弱项。在规定时间内实现剩余贫困人口全部“清零”，监测户返贫和边缘户致贫风险全面消除。三是着力强化增收帮扶措施。继续落实产业扶贫帮扶措施，先建后补，累计补助284万元，充分调动贫困农户发展产业积极性，产业发展带贫机制取得实效。进一步深化新型经营主体与贫困户利益联结机制，利益链接带动贫困户498户，多举措促进贫困户增收致富。四是着力强化转移就业。鼓励外出务工以增加贫困户家庭收入，全镇贫困人口转移就业1420人，其中省外253人，县外省内353人，当地814人。对符合申报外出务工奖补政策的贫困劳动力确保100%享受奖补政策。进一步建立健全镇村公益性岗位人员考核管理办法，切实发挥镇村公益性岗位人员作用。五是着力健全防止返贫致贫机制。紧紧围绕“两不愁三保障”标准，按脱贫“四不脱”要求，严格落实防止返贫致贫动态监测机制。持续关注收入低于国家扶贫标准1.5倍左右的家庭，以及因病、因灾、非义务教育阶段支出过重和受疫情影响严重的家庭，采取临时救助发放或纳入低保动态管理等措施消除返贫致贫风险，多措并举全力降低疫情产生影响，进一步巩固提升脱贫攻坚成果，确保脱贫攻坚战实现圆满收官。六是着力推动各类问题整改清零。常态化跟踪督促问题整改落实，各级巡视巡察发现问题，提出意见建议共76条，涉及问题和整改意见建议全部完成整改，部分问题整改建立长期坚持的保障机制。

脱贫攻坚中，沙溪镇在群众家中以“火塘会”的形式召开群众会议，共商群众脱贫事宜

In the Fight against Poverty, Shaxi Town Holds a Meeting with the Masses in Their Homes in the Form of "Fire Pits" to Discuss Matters of Poverty Alleviation

沙溪镇乡村卫生室　Rural Health Office of Shaxi Township

沙溪镇建立“爱心超市”，激发群众在脱贫攻坚中的内生动力
Shaxi Township Establishes a "Caring Supermarket" to Stimulate the Endogenous Motivation of the Masses in the Fight against Poverty

Section 2 Poverty Alleviation

From 2011 to 2015, Shaxi, in accordance with the goal of poverty alleviation and elimination, took the "Five Measures" as a breakthrough, and launched a new round of fight against poverty. The investment in special projects for poverty alleviation was 8.85 million RMB. Carry out the implementation of Changle, Hualong and Shilong back mountain Yi Nationality natural village whole village promotion project, benefiting the poor people 836 households 2,910 people. Promote the comprehensive development of poverty alleviation in Shaxi Town in Heihui River Area, and issue 23 million RMB interest-bearing loans for poverty alleviation. Solidly carry out the "Focal Point, Responsible, Help"①, "Change Work Style, Go to the Grass-roots Level and Visit Poor Villages and Households"② poverty alleviation work, the state county town to 775 poor households 2,632 people for two rounds of visits, at the same time complete the work of "Follow up and Checks" of poverty registration. In 2015, 89 households and 315 people were lifted out of poverty. Shaxi actively implements the relocation project to alleviate poverty, and the fight against poverty in remote and poor mountainous areas is fully launched.

After 2016, Shaxi Town clings to the target task of one time high-quality poverty elimination and removal, and solidly promotes the poverty alleviation policies and measures to take root with

发展经济作物油菜种植 Developing Economic Crop Rape Cultivation

① Cadres at the provincial, municipal, county, and township levels have worked together as a whole to establish and improve a long-term mechanism for poverty alleviation work at designate points on link poverty alleviation work with "provincial and municipal leaders helping poor areas, county leaders helping poor village, village leaders helping poor households".

② Refers to the establishment of "Focal Point, Responsible, Help" on the basis of a long-term mechanism, the province's unified organization to carry out the "change style of work to go to the grassroots level to visit poor villages and poor households" work.

offensive measures and delicate efforts. In-depth and accurate dynamic management work, from 2016 to 2020, a total of 824 households and 3,244 people were alleviated, six poor villages were out of poverty, and the poverty incidence rate was reduced from 12.44% in 2014 to 0, realizing high-quality one-time overcome poverty. Continuously promoting industrial poverty alleviation, the steady development of advantageous industries such as roasted tobacco, seed corn, Chinese Herbal Medicine and ground ginseng, the steady promotion of tourism industry, the further strengthening of the benefit linkage mechanism between new business entities and poor households, and the more obvious effect of bringing poverty; completing 14 sessions of labor force training for a total of 3,400 people, transferring 3,250 people to the labor force, including 1,199 people transferring to the registered poor households, and handling the "One-time Transportation Subsidy" for 235 registered poor households who is going out to work. The proportion of wage income of the poor people has increased significantly; we have continued to deepen education and health poverty alleviation, 3,244 people in the town completed poverty registration, 100% of the poor people have participated in medical insurance and major disease insurance, and no students in compulsory education have dropped out of school due to poverty; we have fully implemented housing safety guarantee, a total of 325 households completed relocation to alleviate poverty, the implementation of the completion of the four categories,[3] non-four categories of objects of agricultural housing renovation 536 households, housing quality improvement 826 households, the poor people's safe housing problems have been effectively solved; Improve the management system of safe drinking water in rural areas, the comprehensive implementation of household

建设中的长乐后山扶贫安置点　Poverty Alleviation settlement in Changle Back Mountain under Construction

③ 1. rural low-income people; 2. provincial economically weak villages; 3. key areas for poverty alleviation and development; 4. key counties (districts) for poverty alleviation and development.

surveys, water quality testing, facilities supporting, comprehensive improvement and improve the recognition of the "Five Full Coverage "to establish and improve the long-term mechanism of water management and use, the town's safe drinking water is fully guaranteed; strengthen the implementation of the rectification and reform of the problem, the cumulative rectification and clearing of various types of inspections and inspections at the higher level found 190 problems; do realistic and detailed village-level construction drawings and town-level roadmap preparation, the implementation of dynamic adjustment, hanging maps, and efforts to make up for the shortcomings; strengthen propaganda guidance, in-depth implementation of strengthen propaganda guidance, carry out in-depth "Self-improvement, Integrity, Gratitude" publicity and education activities, continue to promote the "Small speaker and big radio, to help fight poverty" project, prepare for the construction of 14 "Benevolence Supermarket", to stimulate the endogenous motivation of the masses and support both the intellect and the will.

In 2020, Shaxi Town passed the third-party assessment and inspection, poverty alleviation census acceptance and effectiveness assessment. Subsequent always adhere to the poverty relief policies continue after Shaxi Town being removed from poverty list and keep "Four Not Take Off"④, focus on the return of poverty monitoring and continuous help, to ensure that poverty alleviation efforts are not reduced, investment is not reduced, the policy remains unchanged. First, raise the political stance, adhere to the poverty alleviation to lead the overall situation of the work, the implementation of the 46 members of the village workforce, the 16 poverty alleviation attack party commando team and the town's cadres and staff to

建好后的长乐后山扶贫安置点 Poverty Alleviation Settlement in Changle Back Mountain Constructed

④ County Party committee secretaries and county mayors should remain steadfast in their posts, and not shirk their responsibilities, major poverty relief policies will continue, and work teams must not withdraw but continue their assistance. Every effort must be made to prevent people from falling back into poverty, supervision must continue.

沙溪华龙村华丛山易地搬迁点　Relocation Site in Huacong Mountain, Hualong Village, Shaxi

fight and win the battle against poverty awareness of responsibility, to ensure that the main energy always focus on the work of poverty alleviation. The second is to focus on the remaining poor people out of poverty. Focus on the "Two Assurances and Three Guarantees" and safe drinking water outstanding problems and poor households out of poverty five standards, according to "A Household a Solution, a Person a Measure" to complete the town 67 households 183 people remaining poor households, 44 households out of poverty monitoring households, 53 households on the edge of the shortcomings and weaknesses. Within the specified time, all the remaining poverty-stricken people were cleared, and the risk of poverty among monitoring households and marginal households was completely eliminated. Thirdly, we focus on strengthening measures to help increase income. Continue to implement industrial poverty alleviation and support measures. First build and then subsidize, the total subsidy of 2.84 million RMB, fully mobilize the enthusiasm of poor farmers to develop industries, industrial development with poverty mechanism to achieve effective results. Further deepen the new business entities and poor households interest linkage mechanism, interest linkage led to 498 poor households, multiple initiatives to promote poor households to increase their income and get rich. Fourth, efforts to strengthen the transfer of employment. Encourage working outside to increase the family income of poor households. 1,420 poor people in the town have been transferred to employment, including 253 people outside the province, 353 people outside the county and 814 people locally. For the poor laborers who are eligible to declare outworking bonus policy, we ensure that 100% of them enjoy the bonus policy. Further establish and improve the assessment and management methods of public welfare post personnel in towns and villages, and effectively play the role of public welfare post personnel in towns and villages. Five is to make efforts to improve the mechanism of preventing return to poverty. Focusing closely on the standard of "Two Assurances and Three Guarantees", according to the requirement of "Four not take off", strictly implement the dynamic monitoring mechanism to prevent returning to poverty. Continuously pay attention to families whose income is less than 1.5 times the national poverty alleviation standard, as well as families whose expenses are too great due to illness, disaster, non-compulsory education and seriously affected by the epidemic, and take measures to eliminate the risk of returning to poverty by issuing temporary assistance or incorporating into the dynamic management of low income security, etc., and take multiple measures to reduce the impact of the epidemic, further consolidate and enhance the results of poverty eradication, and ensure a successful conclusion of the battle against poverty. Sixth, efforts to promote the rectification of various problems to zero. Normalized tracking and supervision of the implementation of the rectification and reform of the problem, inspection at all levels found that the problem, a total of 76 suggestions, involving problems and rectification suggestions all completed rectification, part of the problem rectification to establish long-term persistent guarantee mechanism.

发展经济作物（灯盏细辛） Development of Economic Crops(Erigeron Breviscapus)

第七章

特色沙溪

Chapter 7
Special Shaxi

第一节　特色小镇的创建

沙溪古镇特色小镇规划面积3.14平方千米，核心区范围为原寺登街核心保护区。

沙溪古镇依托悠久的茶马文化、浓郁的白族风情和丰富的旅游资源，大力发展以休闲旅游为主导、文化创意为特色、高原特色农业为辅助的产业体系，重点实施基础设施改造、建筑风貌整治、民宿客栈打造、特色餐饮培育、文化氛围营造和“一部手机游云南”提升等项目，着力将沙溪古镇打造为大滇西旅游环线上的魅力小镇和世界旅游目的地。

沙溪古镇特色小镇项目计划总投资14.29亿元，实施35个项目，分别为公共基础设施建设、产业项目和运营管理类项目3大类别，建设年限2017—2020年。截至2020年底，35个项目已完成建设。

沙溪古镇采取“1+N”模式推进，广东奥园文化旅游投资集团有限公司为沙溪古镇特色小镇投资主体，剑川县人民政府与广东奥园文化旅游投资集团有限公司成立平台公司共同投资经营沙溪古镇。同时，南京先锋书局、中圣明达控股集团有限公司、大理兰林阁等一批有情怀、有实力的知名企业入驻沙溪。

沙溪古镇入口 Entrance to Shaxi Ancient Town

沙溪古镇秉持精雕细琢、精益求精的原则，在打造一流品牌、实施一流管理、提供一流体验上认真谋划，高质量可持续加快沙溪古镇生态化、智慧化、国际化发展。在特色小镇创建中坚持：

一、规划先行。沙溪特色小镇创建始终坚持规划引领，突出城乡融合发展，以人为核心，以产业为支撑，推动特色小镇“多规合一”。在沙溪原有的《沙溪镇总体规划》《沙溪镇区控制性详细规划》《沙溪历史文化名镇保护规划》《沙溪传统村落群保护与发展规划》的基础上，强化规划体系的有效衔接。委托上海同济城市规划设计研究院和昆明理工大学设计研究院本着“把握重点、突出特色，以人为本、以小为美，操作性强”的原则，编制完成《沙溪古镇（特色小镇）发展总体规划》《沙溪古镇（特色小镇）修建性详细规划》，强化“聚而合、小而美”的含金量，确保特色小镇创建起点高、起步稳、视野宽、标准高。

二、坚守红线。合理界定沙溪古镇人口、资源、环境承载力，注重保护重要历史遗存和民俗文化，紧扣沙溪古镇悠久的茶马文化、浓郁的白族风情、优美的田园风光和丰富的旅游资源等，不贪大求全、盲目扩张，不抹旧涂新、拆旧建新。在特色小镇创建过程中，坚守不触碰生态保护红线、不占用永久基本农田、不通过政府违规举债来建设、不搞变相房地产开发 4 条底线，始终坚持传承和弘扬白族本土文化、传统建筑风格，保持小镇田园风光、古朴宁静的历史风貌。

三、打造特色。沙溪古镇特色小镇创建坚持在保护传承历史文脉、白族文化、田园风光的基础上，聚焦“特色、产业、生态、易达、宜居、智慧、成网”7 大要素，发挥比较优势打造精品工程，突出沙溪特色。

传统民居　Traditional Inhabitants

Section 1 Foundation of Specialty Small Town

The plan area of Shaxi is 3.14 square kilometers, and the key core is the original Sideng Street core protection area.

Relying on the long history of Tea-Horse Culture, strong Bai Nationality amorous feelings and rich tourism resources, the Ancient Town of Shaxi vigorously develops the industry system with leisure tourism as dominant, characterized by cultural creativity and plateau characteristics agriculture as auxiliary. Focus on the implementation of infrastructure transformation, architectural style renovation, Inns and hotels optimization, characteristic catering cultivation, cultural atmosphere construction and "Travel around Yunnan with a Mobile Phone" and other projects. To build Shaxi Ancient Town into a charming town and a world tourist destination on the great Western Yunnan tourism loop.

The project of the Specialty Small Town of Shaxi Ancient Town plans to invest 1.429 billion yuan and implement 35 projects, which are divided into three categories: public infrastructure construction, industrial projects and operation management projects. The construction period is 2017-2020. By the end of 2020, 35 projects had been completed.

Shaxi Ancient Town adopts the "1+N" mode to promote. Guangdong Aoyuan Culture and Tourism Investment Group Co., Ltd., is the main investor in Shaxi Ancient Town. Jianchuan County Government and Guangdong Aoyuan Culture and Tourism Investment Group Co., Ltd., set up a platform to jointly invest in and operate Shaxi Ancient Town. At the same time, Nanjing Pioneer Book Company, Zhongsheng Mingda Holding Group Co., Ltd., Dali Lanlinge Company and other sentimental fleelings and well-known companies come to Shaxi.

Shaxi Ancient Town upholds the principle of delicate polish and constantly strive for perfection, carefully plans to create first-class brand, implement first-class management and provide first-class experience, and sustainably speed up the ecological, intelligent and international development of Shaxi Ancient Town with high quality. Adhere to the following in the creation of the Specialty Small Town:

1. Planning comes first. The establishment of Shaxi Specialty Small Town always adheres to planning leadership, highlights the integrated development of urban and rural areas, takes people as the core, takes industry as the support, and promotes the "Integration of Multi-regulations" of the Specialty Small Town. On the basis of the original "Shaxi Town Master Plan", "Shaxi Town Detailed Control Plan", "Shaxi Historical and Cultural Town Protection Plan" and "Shaxi traditional Village Group Protection and Development Plan", strengthen the effective connection of the planning system. Shanghai Tongji University urban planning design and research institute and design institute of Kunming University of science and technology are appointed in line with "Grasp Emphasis, Highlight the Characteristics, People-oriented, Small but Beautiful, High Maneuverability" principle, compiled "Overall Development Plan of Shaxi Ancient Town (Specialty Small Town)" and "Detailed Constructional Planning of Shaxi Ancient Town (specialty small sown)", strengthen the "Poly,

Small but Beautiful", to ensure the Specialty Small Town to create a high starting point, steady start, wide vision, high standards.

2. Stick to the red line. Reasonably define the population, resources and environmental carrying capacity of Shaxi Ancient Town, pay attention to the protection of significant historical relics and folk-custom heritage, pay close attention to the Tea-Horse Culture with a long history in Shaxi Ancient Town, rich Bai Nationality customs, beautiful pastoral scenery and rich tourism resources, etc. Do not seek perfection, expansion blindly, do not change old buildings into new, nor demolish old buildings to build new ones. In the process of establishing the Specialty Small Town, we should adhere to the four bottom lines of not touching the red line of

ecological protection, not occupying permanent basic farmland, not building through illegal borrowing by the government, and not developing real estate in disguise. We always adhere to the inheritance and promotion of Bai national Culture, traditional architectural style, maintain the idyllic scenery and the peaceful historical features of the small town.

3. Create features. On the basis of protecting and inheriting historical cultural, Bai culture and pastoral scenery. Focus on the seven elements of "Characteristics, Industry, Ecology, Accessibility, Livable, Smart and Network", give play to comparative advantages to create high-quality projects and highlight Shaxi Characteristics.

“鱼米之乡”沙溪坝子 "Land of Fish and Rice" Shaxi Basin

永久基本农田保护　Permanent Basic Farmland Protection

云南省省级非物质文化遗产项目白族阿吒力民俗音乐进社区展演活动

Yunnan Provincial Intangible Cultural Heritage Project Bai Nationality Acharya Folk Music Enters into Community Exhibition

特色卫生间　Featured Toilet

观光农业　Sightseeing Agriculture

第二节　特色小镇的发展

2017年列入特色小镇创建名单以后，沙溪古镇始终遵循特色小镇创建标准，坚持“世界一流、中国唯一”的定位，紧盯目标，持续发力，着力打造大滇西旅游环线上的魅力沙溪和世界旅游目的地。

1.坚持项目带动战略。先后完成核心区古建筑修复及活化利用、基础设施改造提升、高端智慧公共卫生间、古镇风貌提升、“一部手机游云南”完善提升、沙溪古镇特色民宿客栈建设、茶马古道文化体验中心项目、古镇绿化提升项目、瑞士庄园（下科湿地公园）、综合环境整治项目建设、生态廊道建设、古镇消防安防设施、特色小镇智能停车体系建设、黑潓江漂流体验、空心村活化利用、南片区主街道建设、沙溪兰林阁特色酒店、沙溪生态田园综合体、沙溪镇鳌凤村乡村振兴试点等。通过项目实施，核心区水、电、路、通信、停车场等基础设施得到全面改造提升，系统完备、高效实用、智能绿色、安全可靠的现代化旅游和市政基础设施体系不断完善。

2.特色文化加快打造。在修复和保护好沙溪古镇历史文化遗存的同时，充分挖掘并向外展示茶马文化、洞经古乐、白族歌舞、民俗节庆等民族文化。完成兴教寺非遗展示、古戏台茶马古道文化研究成果布展、客栈酒店文化植入，茶马古道文化体验中心、欧阳大院修复等项目。积极推行“天天有演出、周周有活动”，洞经古乐、“霸王鞭”等民族文化活动在兴教寺、四方街、东寨门广场等地火热开展。

3.产业培育有力有效。依托沙溪悠久的历史

中外合作项目——茶马古道文化体验中心 Sino-foreign Cooperation Project: The Historic Tea and Horse Caravan Trail Cultural Experience Center

云南省方志馆沙溪茶马古道分馆 Yunnan Provincial Local Records Museum Shaxi Historic Tea and Horse Caravan Trail Branch

文化、浓郁的民族特色和丰富的旅游资源，因地制宜发展文化创意产业，实现低碳休闲和文化创意融合发展，不断推动第一、二、三产业融合发展。注重聚集产业发展高端要素，以低碳环线和生态廊道为轴，布局茶马古道文化体验中心、先锋书局、国际作家写作中心、湿地公园、精品民宿、生态玫瑰园和车厘子采摘园等多样化的功能区和产业基地。至2020年，沙溪古镇特色小镇产业投资占新增投资的比重和社会投资占新增投资的比重均超过50%。

4.智慧建设快速推进。系统推进“一部手机游云南”平台特色功能完善和创新示范项目建设。强化与云南腾云公司合作，对沙溪“一部手机游云南”平台进行全面升级，完善智慧导览、慢直播、智慧厕所、退（换）货中心、智慧停车、人脸识别、诚信平台、投诉平台等信息建设；完成“腾讯翻译君”小程序打造并同步推广，完成3个慢直播改造提升和42家诚信企业的铺码，新建2个慢直播点位，新增13个语音导览点；建成游客服务中心，完善退（换）货监理中心、医疗急救和失物招领等功能。完成AI扫码识景文字和图片收集，正在安装智慧停车场、智慧厕所设备；完成5G+AR情景再现建模、实拍及内容制作，完成兰林阁智慧刷脸酒店房间智慧设备安装；完成3套互动触摸屏内容设计和3套智慧机器人安装；完成国际版APP工具开发和“沙溪古镇锦囊小程序”编制，手绘地图及导游导览语音录制工作正加快推进；完成东寨门树形通信信号铁塔建设。增设8套小型发射基站、1个固定基站和27个5G高速Wi-Fi覆盖点，实现古镇核心区免费5G高速Wi-Fi全覆盖，成为云南省首个“5G古镇”。

截至2020年底，沙溪古镇特色小镇完成投资14.36亿元，重点实施核心区古建筑修复及活化利用、核心区基础设施改造提升、高端智慧旅游公厕建设、古镇风貌整治、“一部手机游云南”提升完善5大类项目，达到沙溪古镇核心区基础设施功能完善、整体风貌协调一致、环境卫生整洁、智慧建设取得突破、产业培育初见成效的效果。

特色小镇创建不仅恢复了沙溪古镇风貌，还提升了沙溪古镇的品质，并成功创建为国家AAAA级旅游景区。2020年5月，沙溪镇、寺登村分别被云南省文化和旅游厅认定为云南省旅游名镇、名村，2021年6月被评为省级旅游度假区。

通过大力发展文化创意产业，打造房车营地、徒步路线、文创体验项目，实现低碳休闲和文化创意的融合发展，民宿旅游、观光农业、民俗体验、生态美食、民族工艺等旅游产业初具规模。全镇有5100余人从事休闲旅游发展相关行业，通过旅游带动第一、二、三产业的融合发展，促进当地农民就近就地就业。2020年，沙溪古镇景区接待海内外游客108.9万人次，实现旅游社会总收入13.1亿元。沙溪的知名度不断提高，逐步成为国内外游客心中的“诗和远方”。

沙溪房车营地　Shaxi RV Campground

黑溏江畔生态廊道　Heihui River Ecological Corridor

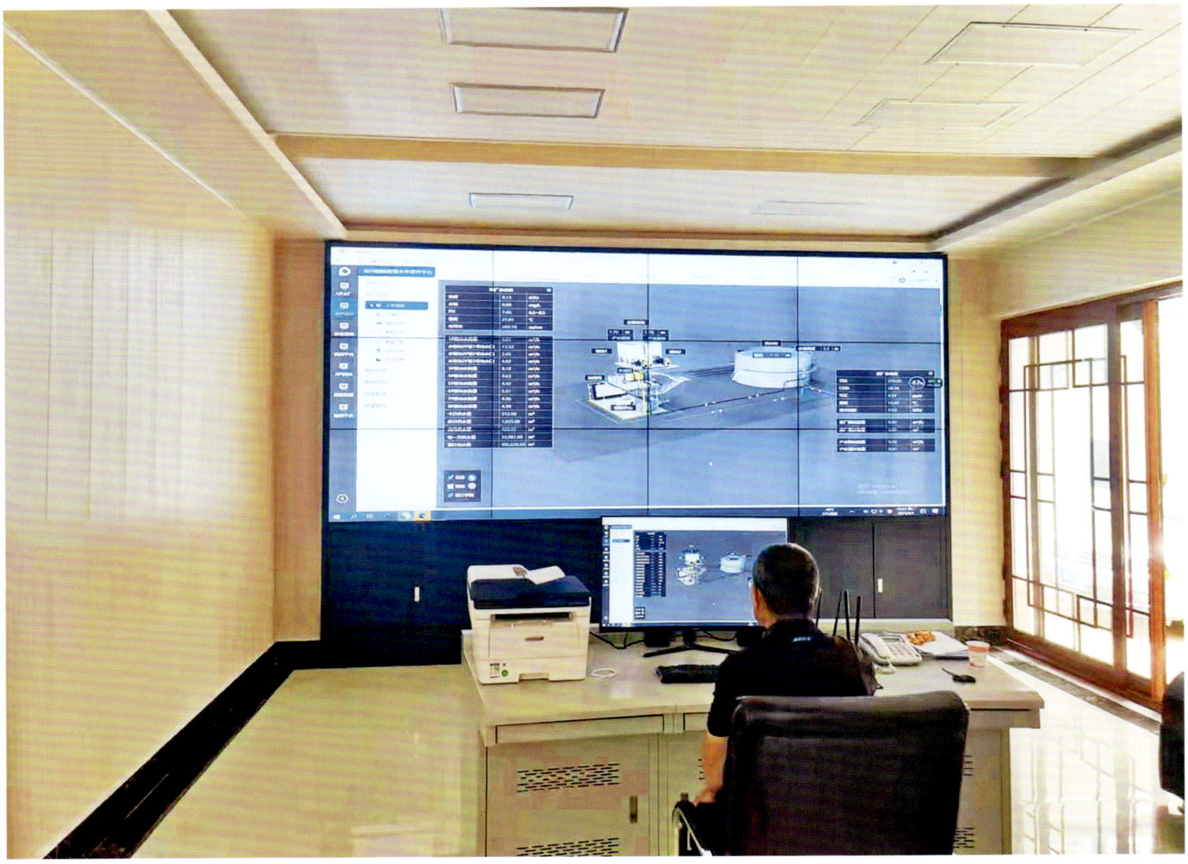

沙溪智慧水务　Shaxi Smart Water Commission

沙溪游客服务中心　Shaxi Tourist Service Center

沙溪绿色停车场　Shaxi Eco-friendly Parking Lot

建设中的沙溪鳌凤游客集散中心　Constructing Shaxi Aofeng Tourist Collection and Distribution Center

沙溪鳌凤游客集散中心效果图　Shaxi Aofeng Tourist Collection and Distribution Center

沙溪特色小镇鳌凤集散中心旅游综合体项目

Shaxi Specialty Small Town Aofeng Collection and Distribution Center Tourism Comprehensive Project

美丽乡村建设　Beautiful Rural Construction

Section 2 Development of Specialty Small Town

In 2017, Shaxi Ancient Town was listed in the list of Specialty Small Town creation. Shaxi Ancient Town always adheres to the standard of Specialty Small Town creation, adheres to the positioning of "World First-class, China's Only", keeps on focusing on the target, make arduous efforts and strives to build Shaxi into a charming town and world tourist destination on the greater West Yunnan Tourism loop.

1. Adhere to the project-driven strategy. Successively completed the core area ancient buildings repair and upgrading activation using, infrastructure renovation, high-end smart public toilet, improving the style of Ancient Towns, "Travel around Yunnan with a Mobile phone" promotion, construction of Shaxi Ancient Town special inns and hotels, the Historic Tea and Horse Caravan Trail Cultural Experience Center project, Ancient Town Greening Improvement Project, Swiss Estate (Xia Ke Wetland Park), comprehensive environmental improvement project construction, Ecological corridor construction, ancient town fire protection and security facilities, construction of smart parking system in Specialty Small Town, Heihui River rafting experience, active and utilization of Hollow Villages, construction of main streets in southern area, Shaxi Lanlinge Characteristic Hotel, Shaxi Ecological Pastoral Complex, and Pilot Projects for Rural Revitalization in Shaxi Town's Aofeng Village, etc. Through the implementation of the project, the infrastructure of water, electricity, roads, communications and parking in the core area has

先锋沙溪白族书局　Shaxi Bai Ethnicity Book Store of Librairle Avant Garde

been comprehensively renovated and upgraded. The modern tourism and municipal infrastructure system with complete system, high efficiency and practicality, smart and green, safety and reliability is continuously improved.

2. The construction of characteristic culture will be accelerated. While restoring and protecting the historical and cultural relics of Shaxi Ancient Town, fully excavate and display the Tea-Horse Culture, Dongjing ancient music, Bai Nationality song and dance, folk festivals and other national culture. Complete the exhibition of the intangible cultural heritage of Xingjiao Temple, the exhibition of the cultural research achievements of the Ancient Opera Stages the Historic Tea and Horse Caravan Trail, the cultural implantation of the inn and Hotel, the cultural experience center of the Historic Tea and Horse Caravan Trail, and Ouyang courtyard restoration, etc. Actively promote "Performances Every Day, Activities Weekly", Dongjing ancient music, "Bawang Whip" and other ethnic cultural activities are popular in Xingjiao Temple, Sifang Street, The East Village Gate Square and other places.

3. Industrial cultivation is powerful and effective. Relying on Shaxi's long history and culture, strong national characteristics and rich tourism resources, develop cultural and creative industries according to local conditions, achieve the integrated development of low-carbon leisure and cultural creativity, and constantly promote the integrated development of the primary, secondary and tertiary industries. Focus on gathering the high-end elements of industrial development, taking the low-carbon loop and ecological corridor as the axis, layout the Historic Tea and Horse Caravan

先锋沙溪白族书局的文创产品 Pioneer Shaxi Bai Nationality Publishing House Cultural and Creative Products

Trail experience Center, Pioneer Publishing House, International Writers' Writing Center, Wetland Park, Boutique Inn, ecological rose garden and cherry picking garden and other diversified functional areas and industrial bases. By 2020, the proportion of industrial investment and social investment in the newly increased investment of Shaxi Ancient Town both exceed 50%.

4. The smart construction is advancing rapidly. Promote the "Travel around Yunnan with a Mobile Phone" platform features improvement and innovation demonstration project construction systematacially. Strengthen Cooperation with Yunnan Tengyun Co., Ltd. comprehensively upgrade Shaxi "Travel around Yunnan with a Mobile Phone" Platform, and improve information construction of smart tour, slow live broadcast, smart toilet, return (Exchange) goods center, smart parking lot, face recognition, integrity platform, complaint platform and so on. Complete "Mr. Translator" mini program creation and synchronous promotion, complete the transformation and promotion of 3 slow live streaming and the paving of 42 honest enterprises, build 2 new slow live broadcast sites, add 13 new voice guide points. And build tourist service centers, improve the functions of return (Exchange) goods supervision center, medical first-aid and lost and found. Complete AI scan code scene recognition text and picture collection, install smart parking lot and smart toilet equipment; complete 5G+AR scene reproduction modeling, live shooting and content production; complete the installation of

干净整洁的街道　Clean and Tidy Streets

smart equipment in Lanlinge Smart Face recognition hotel room; complete 3 sets of interactive touch screen content design and 3 sets of intelligent robot installation. Completed the development of international App tools and the compilation of "Shaxi Ancient Town Tips Mini Program", hand-drawn maps and audio recording of tour guides are being accelerated, and the construction of East village gate tree-shaped communication signal tower has been completed. Add 8 sets of small transmitting base station, 1 fixed base station and 27 5G high-speed Wi-Fi coverage points to achieve free 5G high-speed Wi-Fi coverage in the core area of the ancient town, becoming the first "5G Ancient Town" in Yunnan Province.

By the end of 2020, Shaxi Ancient Specialty Small Town had invested 1.436 billion yuan, focusing on the restoration and activation of ancient buildings in the core area, the renovation and upgrading of infrastructure in the core area, the construction of high-end intelligent tourism public toilets, the renovation of ancient town style and features, and the promotion and improvement of "Tour to Yunnan with Cellphone", 5 categories of projects have been improved. Reaching the infrastructure function of the core area of Shaxi Ancient Town, coordinated overall style, unity and orderly environmental sanitation, breakthrough in smart construction and initial results in industrial cultivation.

The establishment of the Specialty Small Town has not only restored the style and features of Shaxi

引进莎莎玫瑰庄园，实现供销一条龙　Sasha Rose Estate Introduction to Realize One-stop Supply and Marketing

Ancient Town, but also improved the quality of it, and successfully established it as a National AAAA-Level Tourist Scenic Spot. In May 2020, Shaxi Town and Sideng Village were recognized as famous towns and villages in Yunnan Province by the Department of Culture and Tourism of Yunnan Province, and were rated as provincial tourist resorts in June 2021. Through vigorously developing cultural and creative industries, created a RV campground, hiking routes, cultural and creative experience projects, to achieve the integrated development of low-carbon leisure and cultural creativity, residential tourism, sightseeing agriculture, folk experience, ecological food, ethnic crafts and other tourism industries are beginning to take shape. There are more than 5100 people in the town engaged in leisure tourism development related industries, through tourism to promote the integrated development of the primary, secondary and tertiary industries to promote local farmers' local employment. In 2020, Shaxi Ancient Town Scenic Spot received 1.089 million tourists from home and abroad, with a total social income of 1.31 billion yuan. Shaxi's popularity has soared and has gradually become a "Poetry and Distance" in the hearts of tourists at home and abroad.

建设中的鹤剑兰高速公路　Hejianlan Expressway under Construction

寺登街“市网入地”工程　Sideng Street "City Network Access" Project

核心区“古建筑修复及活化利用整治”前 Before the "Restoration, Activation and Utilization of Ancient Buildings" in the Core Area

核心区“古建筑修复及活化利用整治”后 After the "Restoration, Activation and Utilization of Ancient Buildings" in the Core Area

第三节　特色小镇的亮点

沙溪特色小镇建设基于沙溪优美的生态环境、深厚的历史文化资源、良好的产业和新型城镇化发展的基础，以传承和创新发展茶马古道和民族文化遗产为使命，大力发展休闲旅游和文化创意产业，力争建成全国一流、国际知名的特色小镇。

一是建设模式有特色。沙溪在精确把握国际文化遗产保护理念的基础上进一步结合特色小镇的开发建设需要，形成企业主体建设、多方运营管理“1+N”投资模式的亮点工程。

二是产业发展有优势。在发展中，充分结合本土文化遗产特色，依托当地悠久的历史文化、浓郁的民族特色，大力发展文化创意，实现休闲旅游和文化创意的融合发展。

三是特色文化内涵丰富。沙溪保留了传统的白族文化，通过传统古建筑文化、节庆品牌活动、非遗文化交流等传播方式，提高沙溪的知名度，彰显小镇独特魅力。

四是机制政策有创新。规划引领，强化沙溪茶马古道文化特色，坚守红线，打造田园风光的宜居环境，有效传承和弘扬白族本土文化、传统建筑风格，保持小镇田园风光、古朴宁静的历史风貌。

五是创建工作值得借鉴推广。沙溪古镇以传统村落提升改造为起点，充分挖掘民族文化潜力，带动区域内各村落共同发展，促进文旅融合、产村融合，助推脱贫攻坚、助力乡村振兴，这一发展模式对中国古镇和传统村落具有良好的借鉴意义。

Section 3　Specialty Small Town Highlights

The construction of Shaxi Specialty Small Town is based on Shaxi's beautiful ecological environment, profound historical and cultural resources, good industries and the basis of the development of new urbanization, take the inheritance and innovative development of the Historic Tea and Horse Caravan Trail and national cultural heritage as the mission. Develop leisure tourism and cultural and creative industries vigorously, and strive to build a national first-class and internationally famous Specialty Small Town.

1. The characteristic construction mode. On the basis of accurately grasping the concept of international cultural heritage protection, Shaxi further combines the needs of the development and

生态 5G 站　Ecological 5G Station

古镇文创产品（一）　Ancient Town Cultural and Creative Products (1)

古镇文创产品（二）　Ancient Town Cultural and Creative Products (2)

construction of Specialty Small Town, forming a highlight project of enterprise main construction, multi-party operation management "1+N" investment model.

2. Industrial development has advantages. In the process of development, fully combine the characteristics of local cultural heritage, relying on the local history and culture, strong national characteristics, vigorously develop Cultural creativity, and realize the integrated development of leisure tourism and cultural creativity.

3. Characteristic cultural connotation is rich. Shaxi preserves the traditional Bai culture, through traditional ancient architectural culture, festive brand activities, Intangible cultural heritage exchange and other transmission methods, improves the awareness of Shaxi, and highlights the unique charm of the town.

4. Innovations in mechanisms and policies. Take planning as a lead, strengthening the cultural characteristics of Shaxi Historic Tea and Horse Caravan Trail, sticking to the red line, creating a livable environment with idyllic scenery, effectively inheriting and promoting the local culture and traditional architectural style of the Bai Nationality, and maintaining the pastoral scenery of the town and the simple and quiet historical style.

5. The creation is worthy of reference and promotion. Shaxi Ancient Town takes the upgrading and transformation of traditional villages as a starting point, fully digs the potential of national culture, drives the common development of all villages in the region, promotes the integration of culture and tourism, and the integration of rural industries boosts poverty alleviation, and helps rural revitalization. This development model has a good reference significance for ancient towns and traditional villages in China.

四方街乡戏表演　Countryside Opera Performance on Sifang Street

木雕体验　Wood Carving Experience

夜景　Night Scene

助力乡村振兴　Supporting Rural Revitalization

多彩的土地　Colorful Land

绿色停车场　Eco-friendly Parking Lot

特色餐馆　Featured Restaurants

第八章

多彩沙溪

Chapter 8
Colorful Shaxi

第一节　民风民俗

沙溪以农耕文明为主的生产生活方式产生了以农事活动为中心的节日。这些节日可能源于季节更迭、祈求丰收、崇拜英雄，也可能来自谈情说爱、传统习俗、宗教信仰。在沙溪，最重要的节日为春节，其次是最有特色的二月八“太子会”和石宝山歌会，还有火把节、本主会、文昌会、观音会、龙王会等。

Section 1　Local Customs

Shaxi's festivals centered on agricultural activities come from the production and lifestyle based on farming civilization. These festivals may originate from changing seasons, praying for a good harvest, worshipping heroes, as well as love, traditional customs, and religious beliefs. In Shaxi, the most important festival is the Spring Festival, followed by the most distinctive February 8 "Prince's Day" and Mount Mount Shibao Folk Songs Festival, as well as Torch Festival, Local Deity Worship Festival, Wenchang Festival, Guanyin Festival, Dragon King Festival, etc.

沙溪春节文艺活动 Cultural Activities in Shaxi Spring Festival

春节前沙溪群众采购年货　Shaxi People Do New Year Shopping before the Spring Festival

一、春节

沙溪的春节同剑川一样，人们在家门口插上燃烧的双数香，打扫家里和周边卫生，贴好春联，准备丰盛的除夕晚餐。食物特别讲究，煮好猪头猪尾、阉割过的公鸡和鱼，先供奉在楼上祖宗壁龛前或堂屋供桌上；下午准备晚饭前，须到大门口、猪厩前磕头祭奠，然后回到厨房加工晚餐吃的菜肴；正式吃饭前燃放鞭炮，送出当晚吃的食物一碗及酒水各一杯，给没法进家的“饿鬼”享用；吃年饭菜肴中一定要有猪头、猪尾、鱼、粉丝等，寓意有头有尾，年年有余，一家人心连心。晚上要守岁，第二天早上即大年初一到门外或院内燃放鞭炮，烧头香，抢头水，早餐要吃元宵，寓团圆之意。初二起，人们去亲朋好友家拜年，开始扫墓。

贴春联　Paste Spring Couplets

除夕祭品　New Year's Eve Offerings

“打春牛”活动（一） "Fighting the Spring Cattle" Activity (1)

1. Spring Festival

The Spring Festival in Shaxi is the same as that in Jianchuan. People put even numbers burning incense sticks at the gate, clean the house, paste Spring Festival couplets, and prepare a sumptuous New Year's Eve dinner. People pay special attention to the food, cooked pig head and tail, soused chicken and fish, these delicacies are first enshrined in the ancestral alcove upstairs or on the worship table in the central room. In the afternoon, before preparing dinner, people must kowtow to the gate and in front of the pig stable, and then return to the kitchen to cook for dinner. Firecrackers are set off before formal meals and a bowl of food and a glass of wine are given to the "Hungry Ghosts" who can't come back to their home. There must be pig heads, pig tails, fish, fans, etc., in the dishes of the Chinese New Year's dinner, which means that there is a beginning and an end, surplus every year, and the families pull together. It is necessary to keep the New Year's Eve in the evening. And in the next morning (The first day of the Lunar New Year), people set off firecrackers outside the door or in the courtyard, burning first incense, rushing to get the first bucket of water from the well, and eating sweet dumplings for breakfast, which means reunion. From the second day of the lunar new year, people visit relatives and friends to pay New Year's greetings and sweep graves and worship ancestors.

“打春牛”活动（二） "Fighting the Spring Cattle" Activity (2)

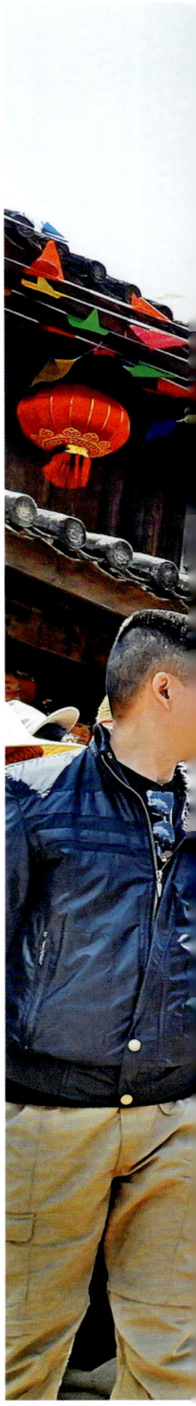

二月八“小太子”　February 8 "Young Prince"

二、二月八“太子会”

二月八“太子会”是沙溪传统重大节庆之一，是当地纪念“太子”出家的民间佛教活动。二月初八这天，沙溪坝十村八寨的群众身着盛装聚集到寺登街上，载歌载舞，举行盛大的纪念活动。几人抬着释迦牟尼“太子”雕像，众人保驾护卫，一路钟鼓齐鸣，焚香诵经，浩浩荡荡地漫游“四门”。村民常常牵儿带孙，把自家孩子装扮成“太子”模样，跟着高台大轿上的太子巡游四门，以祈万事如意、添财进福。

古戏台前游“太子”　Tour "Prince" in front of the Ancient Opera Stage

2. "Prince's Day" on February 8

The "Prince's Day" on February 8th is one of the major traditional festivals to commemorate the "Prince" be a monk in Shaxi. On February 8 in lunar month, people in Shaxi Basin gathered on the Sideng Street in costumes, singing and dancing, and held a grand commemorative event. Several people carried the statue of Sakyamuni when he was a "Prince", and others escorted the guards. Bells and drums sounded, burning incense and chanting all the way, and they roam to the "Four Gates" mightily. Villagers often lead their kids who dress up as "Prince", follow the prince statue on a high platform sedan chair to parade around the Four gates, praying for good luck and fortune.

沙溪古镇接“太子”　Picks up "Prince" in Shaxi Ancient Town

二月八“太子会”上的群众活动　Mass Activities at the "Prince's Day" on February 8

彝族火把节　Yi Nation Torch Festival

三、火把节

火把节是沙溪当地最主要的传统节日之一，每年农历六月二十五日举行。白语称火把节为“付旺吾”，即“六月狂欢节”。沙溪各村各寨在村中竖起大火把，火把上方四周缀满五彩三角旗以及棠梨、火把梨和面塑饰物等吉祥物，顶端扎升斗旗帜，上书“五谷丰登”“风调雨顺”等大字。晚上，大家聚集在大火把下，手举小火把，燃松香粉，以火相燎，“泼火”表示祝福。当年得子嗣之家向全村人发糖果、炒豆，以示“道喜”。人们围着火把唱歌跳舞，弹三弦唱白曲，通宵达旦。

3. Torch Festival

The Torch Festival is one of the most important traditional festivals in Shaxi. It is held on the 25th June in the lunar calendar every year. In Bai language, the Torch Festival is called "Fu Wang Wu", means "June Carnival". The large torches erected in villages of Shaxi. The top of the torches are decorated with colorful triangular flags and mascots such as birchleaf pear, torch pears and dough ornaments. The top of the torches is hoisted with bucket flags with letter "A Bumper Grain Harvest" and "Good Weather for the Crops". In the evening, everyone gathered under the big torches, held small torches in their hands, burned rosin powder, "Splashed fire" to each other to express blessings. At that time, the family which got a baby last year need distribute candies and fried beans to the whole village people to show "Congratulations". People sing and dance around the torches, played sanxian and sang Bai songs all night.

扎火把　Make Torch

竖火把　Put up the Torches

火把节狂欢　Torch Festival Carnival

火把节祭品　Torch Festival Offerings

瑞士苏黎世联邦理工学院遗产保护专家雅克博士（图中饮酒的男士）参加石宝山歌会节
Dr. Jacques, a Heritage Conservation Expert at the Swiss Federal Institute of Technology in Zurich (The Man Drinking in the Picture), Participated in the Mount Shibao Folk Songs Festival

四、石宝山歌会

石宝山歌会是滇西北地区盛大的民族传统节日，每年农历七月最后三天在石宝山上举行。届时，来自剑川、洱源、鹤庆、兰坪、云龙、大理、丽江等三州八县的各族群众身着盛装，身挂龙头三弦，纷至沓来，共迎石宝山歌会。方圆十多里的山间小道上，花枝树丛间，矗岩巨石下，淙淙山泉边，游人如织，男女青年弹响铮铮龙头三弦；歌者对唱悦耳花柳曲，互诉衷肠，歌颂蜜一般甘甜的生活，借此机会结交新友。夜幕降临后，盛大的篝火晚会是歌会的“重头戏”，青年男女耍起石宝山特有的“香龙”，跳起霸王鞭舞，欢歌笑语，弦歌鼎沸，通宵达旦。石宝山歌会有“千年赶一会，一会赶千年”之美誉，2008年被列入第二批国家级非遗保护名录。

石宝山歌会节上的小歌手　Little Singer at Mount Shibao Folk Songs Festival

石宝山歌会节文艺表演　Theatrical Performance in Mount Shibao Folk Songs Festival

石宝山歌会节迎接四方宾客　Mount Shibao Folk Songs Festival Welcomes Guests from all over the World

4. Mount Shibao Folk Songs Festival

The Mount Mount Shibao Folk Songs Festival is a grand traditional national festival in northwestern Yunnan. It is held on the Mount Shibao on the last three days in July in lunar calendar every year. At that time, people of all ethnic groups from Jianchuan, Eryuan, Heqing, Lanping, Yunlong, Dali, Lijiang and other three prefectures and eight counties, dressed in costumes and bring the three-stringed instrument with dragon heads, come in a continuous stream to welcome the Mount Shibao Folk Songs Festival. On the mountain trails with a radius of more than ten miles, among the flowers and trees, under the rocky boulders, and by the gurgling mountain springs, the tourists are countless, and young people play the three-stringed instrument; The singers sing to each other, sue the words from the heart mutually, sing about the life, and take this opportunity to make new friends. After the night falls, the grand bonfire party is the "Highlight" of the singing party. Young men and women play the unique "Incense Dragon" of Mount Shibao, dance the Ba Wang whip dance, cheering and laughing, and sing songs all night long. Mount Shibao Folk Song have the reputation of "Once a Thousand Years, and One Thousand Years Remember". In 2008, Mount Shibao Folk Songs Festival was included in the second batch of national intangible cultural heritage protection list.

民间对歌　Ballad Singing

弦歌传情　Music and Singing Express Feelings

2017 年石宝山歌会节赛歌场景　2017 Mount Shibao Folk Songs Festival Competition Song Scene

2017年石宝山歌会节　2017 Mount Shibao Folk Songs Festival

石宝山歌会节白曲对唱　Mount Shibao Folk Songs Festival Bai Song Antiphonal Singing

情定石宝山　Love in Mount ShiBao

石宝山歌会节沙溪分会场活动 Shaxi Branch of Mount Shibao Folk Songs Festival

五、沙溪集市

集市对沙溪来说有着特殊的意义，沙溪特殊的地理位置使寺登街成为茶马古道上一个重要的物资交流集散地，获得了“茶马古道上唯一幸存的古集市”这一美名。如今，沙溪仍是滇西北片区最重要的大牲畜交易市场之一。集市每个星期五进行，当天一早，群众就会把自家的蔬菜水果、土特产和手工制作的生产生活用品等拿到集市上交易，延续着古老的传统。

5. Shaxi Market Fair

The market has special meaning for Shaxi. The special geographical location of Shaxi makes Sideng Street an important material exchange and distribution center on the Historic Tea and Horse Caravan Trail, and has won the name of "The Only Surviving Ancient Market on the Historic Tea and Horse Caravan Trail". Today, Shaxi is still one of the most important large livestock trading markets in northwestern Yunnan. It is held every Friday, and in the early morning of that day, the masses will bring their own vegetables and fruits, local products and hand-made production and daily necessities to the market for trading, this continues the ancient tradition.

热闹的集市　Lively Market Fair

沙溪集市　Shaxi Market Fair

沙溪集市寻幽探古活动　Exploring the Ancient Activities in Shaxi Market

六、本主节

本主崇拜是白族特有的宗教信仰，本主是本境之护佑与主宰之神。白族聚居的村寨几乎都有本主庙，大多本主庙前建有戏台。本主并非令人望而生畏之神，而是像人一样有七情六欲、有妻室儿女、有亲戚朋友、有婚丧嫁娶之神。本主崇拜按其内容和性质，可以分为自然崇拜、祖先崇拜、英雄崇拜和偶像崇拜等。本主造型古朴生动，富有地方特色。关于本主还流传着许多幽默风趣的轶事。每年本主诞辰都要举行盛大的本主会，时间为1~3天。本主会期间，要举行迎本主仪式，举行唱戏、耍牛、唱白曲等丰富多彩的文娱活动，村民还在家中宴请亲朋好友。

6. Local Deity Worship Festival

The worship of the Local Deity is the unique religious belief of the Bai people. Local Deity is the protector and dominator of this region. Almost all villages inhabited by Bai people have their own temples, and most of them have a stage in front of the temples. The lord is not a daunting god, but like common human being, has emotions and desires, has wives and children, relatives and friends, and has weddings and funerals. The worship of the lord can be divided into nature worship, ancestor worship, hero worship and idol worship according to its content and nature. The shape of the lord worship is simple and vivid, full of local characteristics. There are also many humorous anecdotes circulating about the lord. Every year on the birthday of the lord, a party is held for 1 to 3 days. During this party, a welcoming ceremony will be held, and colorful cultural and recreational activities such as opera, cow playing, and singing Bai songs will be held. Besides, the villagers will also entertain relatives and friends at home.

沙溪本主祭祀活动　Shaxi Local Deity Sacrificial Activities

白族歌舞　Bai Nationality Song and Dance

唱白曲　Sing Songs of Bai Nationality

高山欢舞　Dance in High Mountains

沙溪洞经古乐　Shaxi Dongjing Ancient Music

七、曲艺歌舞

沙溪民族风情独特浓郁，除了民族节庆，民间文艺也丰富多彩。

7. Song and Dance

Shaxi has unique and rich ethnic customs. In addition to national festivals, there are also colorful folk arts.

省级非物质文化遗产项目——白族阿吒力民俗音乐进社区活动

Provincial Intangible Cultural Heritage Project—Bai Acharya Folk Music Enters Community Activities

石龙乡戏　Shilong Township Opera

集体歌舞　Group Singing and Dancing

国家级非物质文化遗产项目——剑川白曲。石龙村民间白曲艺人进行白曲对唱

National Intangible Cultural Heritage Project—Jianchuan Songs of Bai Nationality. Shilong Village Baiqu Artists Perform Baiqu Antiphonal Singing

沙溪“土八碗”　Shaxi "Tu Eight Bowls"

第二节　美食特产

在沙溪，最负盛名的本土菜肴是“土八碗”，是待客和重要节日的美味佳肴。“土八碗”由红曲肉、粉蒸鱼、千张肉、木耳豆腐、水粉丝、酥肉垫竹笋、白芸豆、百合扣肉圆子，共八碗和一个白族传统腊味腌品拼盘，组成一桌菜肴。荤素搭配的“土八碗”，味美可口，色彩丰富，老少皆宜。每道菜都取有美好寓意的美称。红曲肉美称“延年益寿”，粉蒸鱼美称“年年有余”，千张肉美称“千岁平安”，木耳豆腐美称“和和睦睦”，水粉丝美称“情意绵绵”，酥肉垫竹笋美称“舒舒服服”，白芸豆美称“圆圆满满”，百合扣肉圆子美称“百年好合”，拼盘美称为“吉星高照，亲亲爽爽”。

此外，传统手工制作的豌豆凉粉、粉皮、麦芽糖、火腿、泡梨、羊乳饼等食品，以及地参、松茸、蜂蜜、葛根等原生态食品也独具特色。

古宅品美食 Taste Delicious Food in Ancient Houses

乳饼蒸火腿 Steamed Ham with Custard

白芸豆煮火腿 Boiled Ham with White Kidney Beans

松茸　Matsutake

Section 2　Gourmet Specialty

In Shaxi, the most prestigious local dish is "Tu Eight Bowls", it is a delicacy for hospitality and important festivals. "Tu Eight Bowls" consists of red yeast pork, steamed fish with flour, dried beacurd sheet shaped streaky pork, fungus tofu, water vermicelli, crispy meat pads with bamboo shoots, white kidney beans, lily buckled meatballs, a total of eight bowls and a platter of traditional Bai people's preserved products form table dishes. The "Tu Eight Bowls" with meat and vegetables is delicious and colorful, suitable for all ages. Each dish has a auspicious meaning. Red yeast meat is called "Prolonging Life", steamed fish with powder is called "Surplus Every Year", thousand pieces of meat is called "Peace of Thousands Years", fungus tofu is called "Harmony", water vermicelli are called "Lingering Sentiments", crispy pork pads with bamboo shoots are called "Comfortable", white kidney beans are known as "Nothing to Regret", lily buckled meatballs are known as "Be a Harmonious Union Forever", and platters are known as "Good Luck and Success".

In addition, traditional hand-made pea jelly, vermicelli, maltose, ham, pickled pears, goat milk cakes and other foods, as well as original ecological foods such as ground ginseng, matsutake mushrooms, honey, and pueraria, are also unique.

腌鱼　Pickled Fish

地参　Ground Ginseng

羊乳饼　Sheep Milk Cake

炸粉皮　Fried Sheet Jelly

晒粉皮　Sheet Jelly

白饼　Bai Cake

丰收时节　Harvest Season

第三节　传统生活

沙溪坝子中的黑潓江孕育了博大精深的传统农耕文化，从马帮时代过来的沙溪人民和马结下了不解之缘，到现在人们在生产劳动中还频繁地使用马匹，古老的锄头依然坚韧地凿开土地，播下希望的种子。沙溪的土地和勤劳的沙溪人民给予沙溪昨日的辉煌，沙溪人热爱这片土地，从事传统的劳动，坚守昨日的梦想，始终勤劳，创造美好的未来。

Section 3　Traditional Life

The Heihui River in Shaxi Basin gave birth to a broad and profound traditional farming culture. The people of Shaxi who came from the era of caravans forged an indissoluble bond with horses, and now they still frequently use horses in production and labor, and ancient hoes still tenaciously digging the ground and sowing the seeds of hope. The land of Shaxi and the diligent people of Shaxi gave Shaxi its glory. The people of Shaxi love this land, engage in traditional labor, stick to their dreams, and always work hard to create a better future.

播种　Sowing

牧归　Shepherd's Return

传统木雕　Traditional Wood Carving

白族手工艺制品　Bai Nationality Handicraft Products

休憩　Rest

集市　Market

老灶台　Old Cooktop

赶集路上　On the Way to Market Fair

赶集　Going to the Market

传统木蒸笼制作修补手艺人　Traditional Wooden Steamer Making and Repairing Craftsman

第九章

魅力沙溪

Chapter 9
Charming Shaxi

第一节　守护沙溪

2017年以后，剑川县充分发挥党员带头示范作用，积极探索“党建+古镇”保护模式，通过“四个抓好”专项工作，全力做好沙溪古镇保护管理工作。

一是抓好风貌管控，保护小镇文化遗产。认真贯彻落实《沙溪历史文化名镇保护与发展规划》《沙溪古镇保护管理实施意见》，每日对古镇核心区和风貌管控区进行巡查，对区域内进行的建设活动严格管控，保护好沙溪古镇核心寺登街的传统古村落风貌，推动沙溪乡村旅游发展的灵魂——文化遗产保护的阶段性成果得到保护传承。

二是抓好项目建设，完善小镇基础建设。沙溪古镇通过对核心区域的打造，撬动整个片区，以乡村旅游为着力点，进行旅游重点村多元化建设，实现区域内和谐、可持续发展。为切实推动项目的建设，高度重视，由专人负责每日到项目建设点统计项目建设相关数据，与施工方及时沟通交流，确保项目稳步推进。

三是抓好市场整治，营造良好旅游环境。为

古道风貌　Ancient Roads Style

游客营造良好的旅游环境，做好沙溪古镇旅游市场整治工作，保护好沙溪古镇传统古村落风貌，深入开展旅游市场专项整治工作，重点对破坏古镇风貌，与古镇不相协调的摆摊设点、乱摆乱放，商铺牌匾过大、过于鲜艳，过多使用现代材料制作各种宣传牌、灯箱，部分房屋墙体颜色与古镇不协调的情况进行全面整治，营造良好的旅游环境。

四是抓好安全工作，确保小镇安全稳定。层层签订消防安全责任书，确保责任到人。定期检查兴教寺消防系统及各类灯具，确保无消防安全隐患，认真做好检查记录，同时严格执行24小时值班制度。

目前，剑川县正按“彰显特色、打造产业、创新智慧、追求卓越”的工作思路，继续全力以赴抓整改、强巩固、促提升，建立健全长效管理机制，推进沙溪古镇管理运营制度化、精细化、法治化，充分彰显特色小镇“世界范”、“中国风”和“沙溪色”，让古镇焕发新生机。

Section 1 Guard Shaxi

After 2017, Jianchuan County gave full play to the leading role of party members and actively explored the protection model of "Party building + Ancient Town". Through the special work of "Four Grasps", make full effort to do a good job in the protection and management of Shaxi Ancient Town.

Do a good job in the management and control of the style and protect the cultural heritage of the town. Conscientiously implement the "Shaxi Historical and Cultural Town Protection and Development Plan" and "Shaxi Ancient Town Protection and Management Implementation Opinions" conduct daily patrols of the core area of the ancient town and the style control area, strictly control the construction activities in the area. Protect the traditional ancient village style of Sideng Street, the core of Shaxi Ancient Town, and promote the soul of rural tourism development in Shaxi—the phased achievements of cultural heritage protection are protected and inherited.

志愿者打扫卫生　Volunteer Cleaning

Do a good job in project construction and improve the infrastructure of the town. Through the construction of the core area, Shaxi Ancient Town will drive the entire area, focus on rural tourism, and carry out diversified construction of key tourism villages to achieve harmonious and sustainable development in the region. In order to effectively promote the construction of the project and show great attention to it, a special person will be responsible for collecting relevant data of the project construction at the project construction site every day, and communicating with the construction party in a timely manner to ensure the steady progress of the project.

Do a good job in market regulation and create a great tourism environment. Create an excellent tourism environment for tourists, do a good job in rectifying the tourism market of Shaxi Ancient Town, protect the traditional ancient villages and features of Shaxi Ancient Town, and carry out special rectification work in the tourism market. Focus on solving the style and appearance of the ancient town, in-depth development of special rectification work, such as random setting up stalls that are not in harmony with the ancient town, the plaques of the shops are too large and too bright, and too many modern materials are used to make various propaganda boards and light boxes, the color of the walls of some houses is not in harmony with the ancient town, and other questions. Create a beautiful tourism environment.

Do a good job of safety work to ensure the safety and stability of the town. Sign the fire safety responsibility letter leaders at all levels to ensure that the responsibility is on the person. Regularly inspect the fire protection system and various lamps of Xingjiao Temple to ensure that there are no hidden dangers to fire safety, carefully make inspection records, and strictly implement the 24-hour duty system.

At present, Jianchuan County is continuing to go all out to focus on rectification, consolidation, promotion, and establish a sound long-term management mechanism according to the work idea of "Showing Characteristics, Building Industries, Innovating Wisdom, and Pursuing Excellence". To promote the institutionalization, refinement, and rule of law of the management and operation of Shaxi Ancient Town, fully demonstrate the "World Model", "Chinese Style" and "Shaxi Feature" of the Specialty Small Town, and make the ancient town full of new vitality.

清理占道经营　Clearing up the Road Occupancy Operation

针对“服务设施建设和管理不够精细”情况的整改前

Before the Rectification Focus on the Situation of "Inadequate Construction and Management of Service Facilities"

针对“服务设施建设和管理不够精细”情况的整改后

After Rectification Focus on the Situation of "Inadequate Construction and Management of Service Facilities"

针对“外立面风貌不协调”情况的整改前

Before Rectification Focus on the Situation of "Inconsistent Appearance of the Facade"

针对“外立面风貌不协调”情况的整改后

After Rectification Focus on the Situation of "Inconsistent Appearance of the Facade"

第二节　发展沙溪

沙溪特色小镇创建以传统村落提升改造为起点，充分挖掘民族文化潜力，植入民族文化场景体验、特色客栈、遗产保护交流、田园综合体、古旧建筑修复保护利用等新业态，实施“中瑞合作”“新型城镇化”“建制镇示范试点”“古旧建筑保护修复”“特色小镇创建”等项目，辐射带动区域范围内各村落共同发展，促进文旅融合、产村融合，为世界历史文化遗产保护实践探索出一条保护利用与群众脱贫致富相结合的可持续发展之路。

基于传统村落文化特色的乡村振兴。通过全面的顶层设计，基于传统村落和茶马古道的文化特色，推动沙溪经济、社会、文化、生态环境协调发展，以文化引领产业发展，遵循可持续的绿色增长方式以及低碳生活方式，初步形成基于传统村落文化特色的乡村振兴路径。

以村民为主体的发展策略。把维护农民群众根本利益、促进农民共同富裕作为出发点和落脚点，促进产业发展、生态建设、文化建设和社会治理等活动持续、协调进步，凝聚多元文化之魂、民族精神之根、家园乡愁之情。

开放、多元、动态的发展路径。以世界纪念性建筑的普遍认同，彰显中华民族璀璨历史文化，激发国际社会、各级政府、各类企事业单位及社会组织、社会公众的共同关注，建立有机融合、共兴共荣、自信开放、田园牧歌式的发展模式。

魅力沙溪，未来可期！

美丽沙溪　Beautiful Shaxi

Section 2　Develop Shaxi

The creation of Shaxi Specialty Small Town starts from the upgrading and transformation of traditional villages, fully digs the potential of national culture, and implants new formats such as national cultural scene experience, characteristic inns, heritage protection exchanges, pastoral complexes, and restoration, protection and utilization of ancient buildings. Projects such as "China-Swiss Cooperation" "New Urbanization" "Organized Town Demonstration Pilot" "Old Building Protection and Restoration" "Specialty Small Town Creation", etc., drive the development of all villages in the region, promote the integration of culture, tourism, production and village. Explore a way for the practice of world historical and cultural heritage protection, which protects the utilization of sustainable development combined with the people's poverty alleviation.

Rural revitalization based on traditional village cultural characteristics. Through comprehensive top-level design, based on the cultural characteristics of traditional villages and the Historic Tea and Horse Caravan Trail, promote the coordinated development of Shaxi's economy, society, culture, and ecological environment, lead industrial development with culture, and follow sustainable healthy growth and low-carbon lifestyles. A rural revitalization path based on the cultural characteristics of traditional villages has been initially formed.

Development strategy with villagers as the main body. Taking safeguarding the fundamental interests of the peasants and promoting the common

华龙瞰沙溪　Shaxi from Hualong's Perspective

迎接客人　Greeting Guests

星河　Milky Way

prosperity of the peasants as the starting point and ending point, promoting the continuous and coordinated progress of industrial development, ecological construction, cultural construction and social governance, and condensing the soul of multiculturalism, the root of national spirit, and the nostalgia of homeland affection.

An open, diverse and dynamic development path. With the universal recognition of the world's monumental buildings, it highlights the splendid history and culture of the Chinese nation, stimulate the common attention of the international community, governments at all levels, various enterprises and institutions, social organizations, and the public, and establish a pastoral development model with organic integration, co-prosperity, self-confidence and openness.

Charming Shaxi, the future can be expected!

寺登街东寨门 East Village Gate, Sideng Street

戏台雪景　Snow Scene at the Stage

雨中四方街　Sifang Street in the Rain

瑞雪兆沙溪　Auspicious Snow in Shaxi

沙溪田园　Shaxi Pastoral

沙溪华龙村半山咖啡馆　Shaxi Hualong Village Banshan Café

沙溪特色客栈（一）　Shaxi Characteristic Inn (1)

沙溪特色客栈（二）　Shaxi Characteristic Inn (2)

沙溪无人驿站　Shaxi Unmanned Courier Station

游客共享电子图书　Tourists Share E-books

游客体验AI智慧服务导览机器人　Tourists Experience AI Smart Service Guide Robot

古树下兰林阁酒店　Lanlinge Hotel under the Ancient Tree

古镇繁华重现　The Prosperity of the Ancient Town Reappears

酒店智慧选房　Smart Room Selection of Hotel

电子图书　Electronic Books

第三节　邂逅沙溪

沙溪复兴工程保护了沙溪的田园风光和历史文化，修复了古旧建筑和文化遗存，使沙溪这个茶马古道上的古集市逐渐成为中外游客向往的“诗和远方”。特色小镇的创建切实提升了沙溪古镇旅游环境。

随着大丽高速公路的开通，到沙溪的游客逐年增加，不同肤色的人们来到沙溪古镇，或享受沙溪的古朴与宁静，或探寻马帮时代的足迹，或惊叹沙溪古建筑的精湛技艺，或体验白族的民族风情，或观赏沙溪田园风光的自然美丽。沙溪，这个沉寂许久的特色小镇正以一种崭新的姿态走进大众的视野。

Section 3　Meet Shaxi

The Shaxi Renaissance Project has protected the idyllic scenery and historical culture of Shaxi, restored ancient buildings and cultural relics, and make Shaxi the ancient market on the Historic Tea and Horse Caravan Trail, gradually become a "Poetry and Distance" for Chinese and foreign tourists. The establishment of Specialty Small Town has effectively improved the tourism environment of Shaxi Ancient Town.

With the opening of the Dali Expressway, the number of tourists to Shaxi is increasing year by year. People of different races come to the Shaxi

Ancient Town, to enjoy the simplicity and tranquility of Shaxi, or explore the footprints of the caravan era, or marvel at Shaxi ancient architecture exquisite, or experience the ethnic customs of the Bai Nationality, or appreciate the natural beauty of the Pastoral Scenery of Shaxi. Shaxi, a Specialty Small Town that has been quiet for a long time, is entering the public's view with a brand-new attitude.

乡戏表演 Folk Play Performance

写生基地　Sketching Place

画家在沙溪古镇写生　Painter Sketching in Shaxi Ancient Town

留住沙溪歌舞　Keep Song and Dance of Shaxi

四方街漫步　Stroll in Sifang Street

国外康养团体在沙溪进行锻炼　Foreign Health Care Groups Exercise in Shaxi

茶马古道文化体验　The Historic Tea and Horse Caravan Trail Cultural Experience

游客在寺登街观看演出　Tourists Watching a Show on Sideng Street

古镇休闲时光　Leisure Time in the Ancient Town

玉津桥夜景　Night View of Yujin Bridge

画家在四方街进行创作　The Painter Works in Sifang Street

文艺青年聚会沙溪　Literary Youth Gathering in Shaxi

寺登街咖啡店　Sideng Street Cafe Store

漫步寺登街　Strolling in Sideng Street

沙溪之韵　The Rhyme of Shaxi

后 记

《剑川沙溪古镇二十年图志》是由剑川县地方志编纂委员会办公室组织编纂的反映沙溪镇2001—2020年二十年来发展、变化、成就的一部综合性图志。对于图志的编纂工作，剑川县委、县政府，沙溪镇党委、镇政府主要领导高度重视，对总体定位、框架结构、主要内容、编纂原则等方面提出了明确的要求，为图志编纂出版工作创造了良好条件。

图志的图片资料由沙溪镇各部门和有关人员提供，文字资料来源于县志、历年年鉴、沙溪镇各部门工作总结、沙溪镇相关规划和地方志资料等。在编纂过程中，我们参考了部分前辈专家的成果，主要参考书目有：《剑川文史资料选编》，剑川县民族宗教事务局主编的《剑川县民族宗教志》，董增旭编著的《导游剑川》，黄印武编著的《在沙溪阅读时间》，罗杨总主编的《中国名城·云南剑川》，潘鲁生、邱运华总主编的《中国名镇·云南沙溪》等。

图志在编纂出版过程中得到了各级各部门和社会各界人士的大力支持。2021年8月，图志初稿完成后，县地方志办组织相关部门及专家对初稿进行审阅。县保密局、县文旅局、县民宗局等相关部门积极支持、主动配合，对志书修改完善工作提出很好的意见和建议；省志办、州志办相关专家，县内张笑、欧阳子龙、刘文忠、杨应宇、黄印武、张龙福、史玉培，沙溪镇张燮举、杨树林、杨建明、赵爱春等人员，对资料和图片认真审核、反复修改，倾注大量心血，并提出宝贵的修改意见与建议。各部门及专家总体认为该图志图片清晰、资料翔实、反映全面、主题明确。为提高图书作为专业志书和精品志书的需要，经多方征求意见，在相关部门及专家提出修改意见与建议的基础上，又两易其稿对文稿和图片进行修改完善和编排设计。参与图志编纂的相关人员克服了时间紧、任务重、要求高等诸多困难，不畏艰难、主动作为、团结协作，完成了编纂工作任务。由于图志编纂时间紧、任务重、要求高，书中难免存在疏漏之处，敬请谅解。

在图志出版之际，谨向所有关心支持编纂工作的各级各部门和社会各界人士表示衷心的感谢，向为编纂出版付出辛苦劳动的所有人员致以崇高的敬意！

编者

2021年12月

Afterword

"Twenty Years of Jianchuan Shaxi Ancient Town Pictorial Annals" is a comprehensive pictorial annals that reflects the development, changes and achievements of Shaxi Town in the past two decades from 2001 to 2020, which is organized and compiled by Jianchuan Local Pictorial Annals Codification Committee Office. The main leaders of Jianchuan County Party Committee, County Government, Shaxi Town Party Committee, and Town Government attach great importance to the compilation of this pictorial annals, and put forward clear requirements for the overall orientation, frame structure, main contents, compilation principles, etc. It has created good conditions for the compilation and publication of the pictorial annals.

The image information of the pictorial annals is provided by the departments and other relevant personnels of Shaxi Town, and the written materials come from county annals, yearbooks, work summary of various departments of Shaxi Town, relevant planning and local chronicles of Shaxi Town, etc. In the process of compilation, we read some of the achievements of predecessors for reference. The main reference books are "The Select and Compile of Jianchuan Historical Accounts" "Jianchuan County National Religion" edited by the National Religious Affairs Bureau of Jianchuan County, "Guide of Jianchuan" from Dong Zengxu, "Reading time in Shaxi" edited by Huang Yinwu, "Jianchuan, Yunnan-famous city in China" by Luo Yang and "China famous town. Yunnan Shaxi" by Pan Lusheng and Qiu Yunhua, etc.

In the process of compilation and publication, pictorial annals received strong support from all levels of departments and people from all walks of life. In August 2021, after the first draft of the pictorial annals was completed, the county local record office organized relevant departments and experts to review the draft. County Secret Bureau, County Bureau of Culture and Tourism, County Bureau of Civil Affairs and other relevant departments actively support and cooperate, and put forward good opinions and suggestions on the revision and improvement of this pictorial annals. Relevant experts from the Provincial Chronicles Office and the State Chronicle Office, Zhang Xiao, Ouyang Zilong, Liu Wenzhong, Yang Yingyu, Huang Yinwu, Zhang Longfu, Shi Yupei, as well as Zhang Xieju, Yang Shulin, Yang Jianming, Zhao Aichun, and other personnel in Shaxi Town, carefully examined and revised the materials and pictures repeatedly, devoted a lot of painstaking efforts, and put forward valuable opinions and suggestions for revision. And they all think that the picture is clear, the information is full, the reflection is comprehensive, and the theme is clear. In order to improve the need of books as professional annals and high-quality pictorial annals, after soliciting opinions from many parties, and also on the basis of modification opinions and suggestions put forward by relevant departments and experts, the manuscripts were rewritten twice, to edit and complete the words and pictures, to design the composition. The relevant personnel involved in the compilation of pictorial annals overcame many difficulties, such as time urgent, heavy tasks and high requirements. They are not afraid of difficulties, take the initiative, unite and cooperate, and complete the task of compilation. Also due to this difficulties, there is inevitably be omissions in the book. Please forgive us for the inconvenience brought to you.

On the occasion of the pictorial annals publication, we would like to express our heartfelt thanks to all departments of all levels concerning the compilation of the editorial work, and all people who have a hard work of work to compile a lot of respect!

Editors

December 2021